MW01285148

FAMILY MEETINGS JOURNAL

for

_____

From _____ To _____

TSG TOOLS

For

Teaching
Self-Government™

Copyright © 2016 Nicholeen Peck, Teaching Self-Government

All rights reserved.

ISBN-13: 978-1492264385

ISBN-10: 1492264385

Family meetings open up healthy communication with a spirit of love and unity.
Rules: no lectures, no arguments, no attitude problems, no pointing fingers

The Importance of Family Meetings

Family meetings are the core of the family government. These meetings hold the structure of the family together and keep the lines of communication open. At family meetings, every family member has equal voice on family issues. However, parents are still parents. The feeling should be more like a board meeting, with each person understanding his or her position in the family — but coming together to make sure the group is running smoothly.

To read more detail about family meetings, purchase a copy of "Parenting: A House United," by Nicholeen Peck.

Family Meeting Details

Set the Tone

Love in the family meeting gives the meeting purpose and vision, as well as makes the meeting more productive. A productive family meeting runs more smoothly, and decisions are made more quickly.

If someone comes to a family meeting with a bad attitude, stop the meeting before it even starts and focus the family on the feeling in the home. If it involves the whole group, then pray, sing an uplifting song, and have a quick discussion about the behavior. Or, if the behavior only involves one person, then pull that person aside.

Also, if parents meet before the family meeting to discuss topics of concern, it can help them to be unified and calm. There is nothing worse than arguing parents in a family meeting! It's vital to come prepared and be unified.

Frequency of Meetings

Family meetings are best held a minimum of weekly. But when first starting out (or if needed), family meetings can be held daily. It's a good idea to schedule family meetings either before or after something the family would never miss so everyone remembers to attend the meeting.

Keeping Record

This book is designed to keep a record of the family meetings so that in each meeting you can review the previous meeting's notes. It's helpful to review what was previously discussed and decided so that you can easily assess how the family is doing at following any new rulings/decisions or plans.

Topics to be Discussed

In this book you'll find a section titled, "Topics to be Discussed at the Next Meeting." If something comes up during the week that needs to be discussed at the next meeting, write it on the page of topics to be discussed. (TIP: Keep this page paper clipped so you can quickly find it.)

I often ask myself, "What would I do when people try to oppose family rules without a 'Topics to be Discussed' sheet?" If I didn't have this document, I would have to explain why we decided a certain thing every time a child wanted to disagree about it. Now I only have to suggest discussing the topic at family meeting and write the topic on the piece of paper. Adding a date is also a good idea because you could forget to look at your "Topics to be Discussed" sheet one time, and the person who had the grievance might forget to bring up the topic. In this case you might come across the notation and not remember if the topic ever got discussed — or when it was written on the idea list.

Topics to be Discussed (continued)

Writing an issue in the "Topics To Be Discussed" section can also make an issue completely disappear. Someone might really want to talk about something that's bothering him or her concerning another person, a chore or a consequence. Because it's the kind of issue that's discussed in family meeting but requires waiting until the next meeting, the issue could be forgotten or become unimportant just by adding it to the "Topics to be Discussed" sheet — where it will wait until the next meeting.

Meeting Length

On the Family Meeting forms, there's a place to note your beginning and ending time. We have these lines on the form to make sure the meeting doesn't go too long. The family meeting should not exceed 20 minutes. If the meeting is too long it could turn into a family fight. Immature people and children can't effectively sit and discuss longer than about 20 minutes.

Also, having the meeting run effectively is more important than resolving every topic suggested for discussion. The point of the family meeting is the feeling of the home, so the family meeting can't get side tracked by conquering every issue presented at a given meeting. If too many issues are suggested for discussion, then it will be necessary to have another meeting another day — preferably the next day.

Have mercy on the attention span of your family; keep track of the time of your meetings.

Who's In Charge?

Every person in the family takes turns leading the family meetings. Write their name in the "Led by" section. Leading an effective meeting is a great life skill. If your children practice leading family meetings for years of their lives, they will be ready to step up and lead other things too.

For the first couple of family meetings the parents should lead the meeting to show how a proper meeting is led. Then, each child in the family gets to have a turn leading the meeting. Be sure to be fair. Give even the littlest ones a chance to lead the meetings. They may only say the words "announcements" and "topics," but they get to feel like they led the meeting. Mom and Dad can help with voting and writing the form. Be sure to complete the "Family Meeting" forms every meeting. If you don't have decisions in writing, they could be disputed and overruled. Even though Mom and Dad are going to lead the first few meetings, make sure you tell your children that they will all get a chance to lead the meetings, and that it's important they watch your example closely on how to be the leader of a meeting.

Write the Date

The "date" line is where the person recording the meeting writes what day the meeting occurred. This is very useful because sometimes someone will say that he or she doesn't remember a certain negative consequence being decided. At this point, you can go to your book and say, "Oh, here it is... a person has to clean the toilet inside and out if they choose not to flush the toilet when they leave the room. This meeting happened just yesterday. I guess it really was decided." A date on a piece of paper makes this paper more of an official document instead of just an idea.

The first thing the leader says in the meeting is, "This [NAME OF YOUR FAMILY] family meeting is now in session on May 20, 2016, beginning at 1:30 p.m." This will be your opening statement. Of course, feel free to change it up a bit to fit your own style. In our family, we just like to have fun being "official." It's all done in good humor.

Announcements

"Announcements" is the second thing that the person leading the meeting says. At this time, each family member takes a turn telling exciting bits of news or giving reminders about events scheduled for the upcoming week. This should only take a couple of minutes, but it's so important! If people have a place to share exciting things from their life or other family member's lives, then the family becomes excited together, which creates unity.

Also, by reviewing the weekly schedule of events together, your family has a weekly plan. This plan creates happiness and security for the whole family throughout the week.

Plan together helps us better prioritize our lives and have more quality family time. For the record, I believe *quantity* of family time to be *quality* of family time. If we don't schedule a certain amount of family time together, the quality of our family relationships decreases.

Topics

After the announcement section of the meeting the person leading the meeting says, "Topics." This part usually takes the most time. Members of the family suggest topics for discussion that affect the whole family, such as: family activities, family problems, chores, standards, motivational systems and consequences. Everyone gets a chance to propose a topic. Even the smallest children should be asked if they have a topic to discuss.

Every person doesn't necessarily have to have a topic for discussion every week. The meeting is just the time to bring up any topics of concern. To have a place where anything can be discussed in a calm, productive way as a group is good for healthy communication. Parents: You're responsible for keeping the meeting calm and productive.

Don't allow people to take off on tangents during the meeting. And don't you take off on tangents either! If parents talk too much during the topics portion of the meeting, the family meeting could turn into a lecture. Family meetings are not the place to lay down the law and be overly critical. Also, remember that when a meeting starts going wrong, it's usually because someone is being selfish. If there is a feeling of selfishness in the meeting, the family will not have a united feeling during and after the meeting. No lectures, no arguments, no attitude problems, and no pointing fingers. These rules apply to children and adults.

Note that we have only included space for 2 topics to be discussed on each Family Meeting page. There are two reasons for this: 1) Some topics will not need to be discussed in the format provided, so you might write your notes under the "Additional Notes" section. 2) In family meetings where you do need to discuss rationals, propose suggestions, vote on those suggestions, and address the decision and benefit to the family, you likely will not have time for more than 2 topics in that meeting. In this case, write down other topics on the next page in the "Topics to be Discussed at the Next Meeting" page and schedule another meeting soon (perhaps the next day) where you can address those topics.

No Pointing Fingers

When a group meets to discuss problems, they must work together as a group. No pointing fingers. Teach your children to describe in general terms the problems they think need to be addressed. We say things like, "I've noticed…" or "Our family seems to have a problem with…." By speaking this way, our family meeting doesn't ever start attacking one person. We don't want a family fight. Pointing fingers leads to family fights.

Rationales

When a topic is brought to the attention of the group, there has to be a reason for addressing the topic. It needs to be important to the group. To remind the family that topics need to be relevant to the whole family, the next line on the family meeting form is the "rationales" line. Each person presenting a topic, except the little ones, need to know why the family would want to discuss the proposed topic. A person should be encouraged to present a topic similarly to this, "I've noticed that our family is having a hard time remembering to clear their dishes after meals. When people decide not to clean up after themselves, it makes our environment messy and it gets other people upset when they have to clean up after someone else. To keep our family relationships happy, I think we should all take our dishes over to the sink after meals."

Suggestions

Following this topic description and rationale, the meeting leader would say, "Dad, what do you propose we should do about this problem?" The person who brought up the topic, who was Dad in this case, is then given the first opportunity to present a solution for the problem. After Dad's proposal, the leader of the meeting says, "What other ideas do we have for encouraging our family to take dishes to the sink after meal times?" Then other ideas are suggested. The person the meeting leader writes down who had suggestions and what they were (we've included spaces for up to 4 suggestions).

Voting Time

The next section of the family meeting form is the family input section simply labeled, "Vote." In this section, a vote is taken and the number of "yes" and "no" votes are counted and recorded for each option (a space to write the vote count is included).

Once the vote has been taken, the leader of the meeting writes down the decision about the issue and the positive or negative consequence that is attached to it. In this case we decided the decision was, "Everyone has to take their dishes to the sink after meals." The consequence is, "If someone doesn't take dishes over on time, that person earns an extra chore." To fit in the space we might simply write, "Dishes in sink after meals on time or extra chore."

Words For Thought

Below are words that we encourage our children to use for rationales. We also talk about these words when we talk about what decision we should choose for our home.

Fair

I've observed that people who get too caught up on making things fair at home have a tendency to create very selfish, whiny children. Making life too fair destroys children.

Entitlement

The flip side of fair is entitlement. Entitlement is a belief that one is deserving of certain privileges or rights. Instead, teach children that they get to choose their own successes and failures and that no one has the responsibility to bail them out of bad situations. However, also teach children to be charitable and give to those who are in need, because that is the way God would have us take care of each other.

Since everyone feels fairness is important, we try to make the decisions in our home as fair as possible. When we choose a negative consequence, the consequence applies to everyone, not just one person. This IS fair. If one person has to have their chores done by breakfast time, then everyone has to have chores done by breakfast time. The time a chore can take can be made fair, but the difficulty of chores cannot be made fair because each person has a different skill level.

Keep fairness in mind, but also keep it in perspective. Trying to have fairness can show concern, but it can also make a person selfish.

Effective

Being effective is a great reason to make a change in the home. Effective means: "Producing a result or causing a result, especially the desired or intended result." If we wake up on time, we are effective in starting our day off well. If we weed the garden 15 minutes daily, we will effectively keep the garden weed free. Groups of people, especially families, are often concerned about being able to effectively run the home and build strong relationships.

Concern

A loving family shows concern for each other. Showing concern is a great reason to make a change in a family or group. Putting perishable food in the refrigerator when you're done using it shows concern for the whole family because you're making sure that other people have fresh food to eat and you are conserving money. Saying you're sorry when you have hurt another person's feelings shows you're concerned about how someone else feels. Showing concern for others is a great reason to make a change at home.

Pleasant

Making the home a pleasant place is always a good reason to change the way something is being done at home. If the home feels pleasant, then the feeling of love and acceptance can be present. A home that's disorderly and distracting because of unpleasant sights, smells or sounds creates anxious, stressful feelings for all family members.

Using and defining these and other words in family meetings will teach your children to think of other people besides themselves. A child who overcomes her natural tendency to be selfish by regularly seeing how actions affect a group of people will be more secure and a great asset to family, community and country. Plus, secure children are happy children.

The Benefit

For each topic there is a line where you can write the benefit. On this line we write how our home will improve from the decision that's been made. If the leader can't think of another reason for making a change in the home, then we encourage the leader to write a sentence that uses one of these words: fair, effective, concern, pleasant, peace, communication, order justice, freedom, or safety.

14 Tips for Successful Family Meetings

1. Don't correct negative behaviors during a family meeting. If someone is having a behavior problem during a meeting, simply say, "[NAME OF PERSON], you're pouting right now. We will need to talk about this after the meeting. Please stay after the meeting for a few minutes to talk with me." If the person doesn't calm down, or becomes out of control, then you may have to adjourn the meeting until she chooses to be in control. Be sure to make a note of where you left off so you know where to begin as soon as you can resume the meeting.

2. Effective family meetings make lasting changes in family government and create strong family relationships. Start effective communication before your children can even talk. If you do that, then they will be used to and master meetings, family government, and good communication.

3. If the children don't like to communicate in family meetings their attitudes are probably red flags that your family communication needs some work.

4. Keeping the meetings to 20 minutes keeps everyone liking and engaged in the meetings.

5. STARTING OUT – At the first family meeting, start creating a family mission statement, and then address what the family wants to do for a family activity. This is a good way to let the children know that family meetings are supposed to make home a fun/happy place. At the next meeting, start bringing up topics about how to fix things at home. In the beginning you may want to have multiple family meetings weekly. After a while you'll get to the point where your meetings will mostly be about the next family activity.

6. Remember to meet at least weekly! If you have weekly family meetings, the whole family will stay focused on their family government. See what happens when you miss a few weeks. The repercussions are noticeable.

7. At family meetings, every family member has equal voice on family issues. However, parents are still in charge of the home. Children don't get to take control of the family. It's not "Animal Farm." Rather, it's more like a board meeting. Each person has their position, but each family member all come together to make sure that the group is running smoothly.

8. Never give negative consequences during a meeting. Instead, simply say, "[NAME OF PERSON], you'll need to stay after the meeting to talk to me for a few minutes." This will keep your meeting running smoothly.

9. DO NOT USE THIS TIME TO LAY DOWN THE LAW OR OVERLOAD CRITICISM.

10. Everyone takes a turn conducting meetings. This is great practice in government skills and gives a feeling of unity to the family, as well as builds the child's self-esteem.

11. When bringing up a topic, don't point fingers. Work as a group; not against any one person. The family must feel united in meeting. The person at fault knows he or she did it anyway. There's no need to draw negative attention to a family member.

12. When suggesting a solution to a topic, teach the children that they also need to present a rational for wanting that solution.

13. Teach proper voting skills and try to be fair.

14. Use this book for reference and a place to keep your "Topics to be Discussed" list so that ideas for meetings are remembered.

TOPICS TO BE DISCUSSED AT THE NEXT MEETING

	Date / Name	Topic

ADDITIONAL NOTES

FAMILY MEETING
Creating Healthy Family Communication

Time Began: _____ Ended: _____ Led by: _____ Date: _____

Announcements: _____

_____

_____

Topic Examples: Family activities, family problems, standards, motivational systems, and consequences.

Rules: No pointing fingers, name calling, etc. Topics should never target a person. Those issues can be discussed in mentor meetings. When discussing rationales, decisions and benefits, keep top-of-mind: Fair, effective, love and concern, pleasant atmosphere.

Topic 1: _____ Rationales: _____

Suggestions:

1. _____   2. _____

_____   _____

3. _____   4. _____

_____   _____

Vote   1. Yes __ / No __   2. Yes __ / No __   3. Yes __ / No __   4. Yes __ / No __

Decision: _____   Benefit: _____

Topic 2: _____ Rationales: _____

Suggestions:

1. _____   2. _____

_____   _____

3. _____   4. _____

_____   _____

Vote   1. Yes __ / No __   2. Yes __ / No __   3. Yes __ / No __   4. Yes __ / No __

Decision: _____   Benefit: _____

Family Meetings should create a tone of peace, communication, order, justice, freedom and safety.

TOPICS TO BE DISCUSSED AT THE NEXT MEETING

	Date / Name	Topic

ADDITIONAL NOTES

_____

_____

_____

_____

_____

_____

_____

_____

_____

FAMILY MEETING
Creating Healthy Family Communication

Time Began: _____ Ended: _____ Led by: _____ Date: _____

Announcements: _____

_____

_____

Topic Examples: Family activities, family problems, standards, motivational systems, and consequences.

Rules: No pointing fingers, name calling, etc. Topics should never target a person. Those issues can be discussed in mentor meetings. When discussing rationales, decisions and benefits, keep top-of-mind: Fair, effective, love and concern, pleasant atmosphere.

Topic 1: _____ Rationales: _____

Suggestions:

1. _____ 2. _____

_____ _____

3. _____ 4. _____

_____ _____

Vote   1. Yes __ / No __   2. Yes __ / No __   3. Yes __ / No __   4. Yes __ / No __

Decision: _____ Benefit: _____

Topic 2: _____ Rationales: _____

Suggestions:

1. _____ 2. _____

_____ _____

3. _____ 4. _____

_____ _____

Vote   1. Yes __ / No __   2. Yes __ / No __   3. Yes __ / No __   4. Yes __ / No __

Decision: _____ Benefit: _____

Family Meetings should create a tone of peace, communication, order, justice, freedom, and safety

TOPICS TO BE DISCUSSED AT THE NEXT MEETING

	Date / Name	Topic

ADDITIONAL NOTES

FAMILY MEETING
Creating Healthy Family Communication

Time Began: _____ Ended: _____ Led by: _____ Date: _____

Announcements: _____

_____

_____

Topic Examples: Family activities, family problems, standards, motivational systems, and consequences.

Rules: No pointing fingers, name calling, etc. Topics should never target a person. Those issues can be discussed in mentor meetings. When discussing rationales, decisions and benefits, keep top-of-mind: Fair, effective, love and concern, pleasant atmosphere.

Topic 1: _____ Rationales: _____

Suggestions:

1. _____ 2. _____

_____ _____

3. _____ 4. _____

_____ _____

Vote   1. Yes __ / No __   2. Yes __ / No __   3. Yes __ / No __   4. Yes __ / No __

Decision: _____ Benefit: _____

Topic 2: _____ Rationales: _____

Suggestions:

1. _____ 2. _____

_____ _____

3. _____ 4. _____

_____ _____

Vote   1. Yes __ / No __   2. Yes __ / No __   3. Yes __ / No __   4. Yes __ / No __

Decision: _____ Benefit: _____

Family Meetings should create a tone of peace, communication, order, justice, freedom, and safety

TOPICS TO BE DISCUSSED AT THE NEXT MEETING

	Date / Name	Topic

ADDITIONAL NOTES

FAMILY MEETING
Creating Healthy Family Communication

Time Began: _____ Ended: _____ Led by: _____ Date: _____

Announcements: _____

_____

_____

Topic Examples: Family activities, family problems, standards, motivational systems, and consequences.

Rules: No pointing fingers, name calling, etc. Topics should never target a person. Those issues can be discussed in mentor meetings. When discussing rationales, decisions and benefits, keep top-of-mind: Fair, effective, love and concern, pleasant atmosphere.

Topic 1: _____ Rationales: _____

Suggestions:
1. _____ 2. _____

_____ _____

3. _____ 4. _____

_____ _____

Vote   1. Yes __ / No __   2. Yes __ / No __   3. Yes __ / No __   4. Yes __ / No __

Decision: _____ Benefit: _____

Topic 2: _____ Rationales: _____

Suggestions:
1. _____ 2. _____

_____ _____

3. _____ 4. _____

_____ _____

Vote   1. Yes __ / No __   2. Yes __ / No __   3. Yes __ / No __   4. Yes __ / No __

Decision: _____ Benefit: _____

Family Meetings should create a tone of peace, communication, order, justice, freedom, and safety

TOPICS TO BE DISCUSSED AT THE NEXT MEETING

	Date / Name	Topic

ADDITIONAL NOTES

_____

_____

_____

_____

_____

_____

_____

_____

_____

_____

FAMILY MEETING
Creating Healthy Family Communication

Time Began: _____ Ended: _____ Led by: _____ Date: _____

Announcements: _____

_____

_____

Topic Examples: Family activities, family problems, standards, motivational systems, and consequences.

Rules: No pointing fingers, name calling, etc. Topics should never target a person. Those issues can be discussed in mentor meetings. When discussing rationales, decisions and benefits, keep top-of-mind: Fair, effective, love and concern, pleasant atmosphere.

Topic 1: _____ Rationales: _____

Suggestions:

1. _____ 2. _____

3. _____ 4. _____

Vote   1. Yes __ / No __   2. Yes __ / No __   3. Yes __ / No __   4. Yes __ / No __

Decision: _____ Benefit: _____

Topic 2: _____ Rationales: _____

Suggestions:

1. _____ 2. _____

3. _____ 4. _____

Vote   1. Yes __ / No __   2. Yes __ / No __   3. Yes __ / No __   4. Yes __ / No __

Decision: _____ Benefit: _____

Family Meetings should create a tone of peace, communication, order, justice, freedom, and safety

TOPICS TO BE DISCUSSED AT THE NEXT MEETING

	Date / Name	Topic

ADDITIONAL NOTES

FAMILY MEETING
Creating Healthy Family Communication

Time Began: _____ Ended: _____ Led by: _____ Date: _____

Announcements: _____

_____

_____

Topic Examples: Family activities, family problems, standards, motivational systems, and consequences.

Rules: No pointing fingers, name calling, etc. Topics should never target a person. Those issues can be discussed in mentor meetings. When discussing rationales, decisions and benefits, keep top-of-mind: Fair, effective, love and concern, pleasant atmosphere.

Topic 1: _____ Rationales: _____

Suggestions:

1. _____ 2. _____

_____ _____

3. _____ 4. _____

_____ _____

Vote   1. Yes __ / No __   2. Yes __ / No __   3. Yes __ / No __   4. Yes __ / No __

Decision: _____ Benefit: _____

Topic 2: _____ Rationales: _____

Suggestions:

1. _____ 2. _____

_____ _____

3. _____ 4. _____

_____ _____

Vote   1. Yes __ / No __   2. Yes __ / No __   3. Yes __ / No __   4. Yes __ / No __

Decision: _____ Benefit: _____

Family Meetings should create a tone of peace, communication, order, justice, freedom, and safety

TOPICS TO BE DISCUSSED AT THE NEXT MEETING

	Date / Name	Topic

ADDITIONAL NOTES

FAMILY MEETING
Creating Healthy Family Communication

Time Began: _____ Ended: _____ Led by: _____ Date: _____

Announcements: _____

_____

_____

Topic Examples: Family activities, family problems, standards, motivational systems, and consequences.

Rules: No pointing fingers, name calling, etc. Topics should never target a person. Those issues can be discussed in mentor meetings. When discussing rationales, decisions and benefits, keep top-of-mind: Fair, effective, love and concern, pleasant atmosphere.

Topic 1: _____   Rationales: _____

Suggestions:
1. _____   2. _____

3. _____   4. _____

Vote   1. Yes __ / No __   2. Yes __ / No __   3. Yes __ / No __   4. Yes __ / No __

Decision: _____   Benefit: _____

Topic 2: _____   Rationales: _____

Suggestions:
1. _____   2. _____

3. _____   4. _____

Vote   1. Yes __ / No __   2. Yes __ / No __   3. Yes __ / No __   4. Yes __ / No __

Decision: _____   Benefit: _____

Family Meetings should create a tone of peace, communication, order, justice, freedom, and safety

TOPICS TO BE DISCUSSED AT THE NEXT MEETING

	Date / Name	Topic

ADDITIONAL NOTES

FAMILY MEETING
Creating Healthy Family Communication

Time Began: _____ Ended: _____ Led by: _____ Date: _____

Announcements: _____

_____

_____

Topic Examples: Family activities, family problems, standards, motivational systems, and consequences.

Rules: No pointing fingers, name calling, etc. Topics should never target a person. Those issues can be discussed in mentor meetings. When discussing rationales, decisions and benefits, keep top-of-mind: Fair, effective, love and concern, pleasant atmosphere.

Topic 1: _____ Rationales: _____

Suggestions:

1. _____ 2. _____

_____ _____

3. _____ 4. _____

_____ _____

Vote   1. Yes __ / No __   2. Yes __ / No __   3. Yes __ / No __   4. Yes __ / No __

Decision: _____ Benefit: _____

Topic 2: _____ Rationales: _____

Suggestions:

1. _____ 2. _____

_____ _____

3. _____ 4. _____

_____ _____

Vote   1. Yes __ / No __   2. Yes __ / No __   3. Yes __ / No __   4. Yes __ / No __

Decision: _____ Benefit: _____

Family Meetings should create a tone of peace, communication, order, justice, freedom, and safety

TOPICS TO BE DISCUSSED AT THE NEXT MEETING

	Date / Name	Topic

ADDITIONAL NOTES

FAMILY MEETING
Creating Healthy Family Communication

Time Began: _____ Ended: _____ Led by: _____ Date: _____

Announcements: _____

_____

_____

Topic Examples: Family activities, family problems, standards, motivational systems, and consequences.

Rules: No pointing fingers, name calling, etc. Topics should never target a person. Those issues can be discussed in mentor meetings. When discussing rationales, decisions and benefits, keep top-of-mind: Fair, effective, love and concern, pleasant atmosphere.

Topic 1: _____   Rationales: _____

Suggestions:

1. _____   2. _____

_____   _____

3. _____   4. _____

_____   _____

Vote   1. Yes __ / No __   2. Yes __ / No __   3. Yes __ / No __   4. Yes __ / No __

Decision: _____   Benefit: _____

Topic 2: _____   Rationales: _____

Suggestions:

1. _____   2. _____

_____   _____

3. _____   4. _____

_____   _____

Vote   1. Yes __ / No __   2. Yes __ / No __   3. Yes __ / No __   4. Yes __ / No __

Decision: _____   Benefit: _____

Family Meetings should create a tone of peace, communication, order, justice, freedom, and safety

TOPICS TO BE DISCUSSED AT THE NEXT MEETING

	Date / Name	Topic

ADDITIONAL NOTES

FAMILY MEETING
Creating Healthy Family Communication

Time Began: _____ Ended: _____ Led by: _____ Date: _____

Announcements: _____

_____

_____

Topic Examples: Family activities, family problems, standards, motivational systems, and consequences.

Rules: No pointing fingers, name calling, etc. Topics should never target a person. Those issues can be discussed in mentor meetings. When discussing rationales, decisions and benefits, keep top-of-mind: Fair, effective, love and concern, pleasant atmosphere.

Topic 1: _____ Rationales: _____

Suggestions:
1. _____ 2. _____

_____ _____

3. _____ 4. _____

_____ _____

Vote   1. Yes __ / No __   2. Yes __ / No __   3. Yes __ / No __   4. Yes __ / No __

Decision: _____ Benefit: _____

Topic 2: _____ Rationales: _____

Suggestions:
1. _____ 2. _____

_____ _____

3. _____ 4. _____

_____ _____

Vote   1. Yes __ / No __   2. Yes __ / No __   3. Yes __ / No __   4. Yes __ / No __

Decision: _____ Benefit: _____

Family Meetings should create a tone of peace, communication, order, justice, freedom, and safety

TOPICS TO BE DISCUSSED AT THE NEXT MEETING

	Date / Name	Topic

ADDITIONAL NOTES

FAMILY MEETING
Creating Healthy Family Communication

Time Began: _____ Ended: _____ Led by: _____ Date: _____

Announcements: _____

_____

_____

Topic Examples: Family activities, family problems, standards, motivational systems, and consequences.

Rules: No pointing fingers, name calling, etc. Topics should never target a person. Those issues can be discussed in mentor meetings. When discussing rationales, decisions and benefits, keep top-of-mind: Fair, effective, love and concern, pleasant atmosphere.

Topic 1: _____ Rationales: _____

Suggestions:
1. _____   2. _____

_____   _____

3. _____   4. _____

_____   _____

Vote   1. Yes __ / No __   2. Yes __ / No __   3. Yes __ / No __   4. Yes __ / No __

Decision: _____ Benefit: _____

Topic 2: _____ Rationales: _____

Suggestions:
1. _____   2. _____

_____   _____

3. _____   4. _____

_____   _____

Vote   1. Yes __ / No __   2. Yes __ / No __   3. Yes __ / No __   4. Yes __ / No __

Decision: _____ Benefit: _____

Family Meetings should create a tone of peace, communication, order, justice, freedom, and safety

TOPICS TO BE DISCUSSED AT THE NEXT MEETING

	Date / Name	Topic

ADDITIONAL NOTES

FAMILY MEETING
Creating Healthy Family Communication

Time Began: _____ Ended: _____ Led by: _____ Date: _____

Announcements: _____

_____

_____

Topic Examples: Family activities, family problems, standards, motivational systems, and consequences.

Rules: No pointing fingers, name calling, etc. Topics should never target a person. Those issues can be discussed in mentor meetings. When discussing rationales, decisions and benefits, keep top-of-mind: Fair, effective, love and concern, pleasant atmosphere.

Topic 1: _____   Rationales: _____

Suggestions:

1. _____   2. _____

_____   _____

3. _____   4. _____

_____   _____

Vote   1. Yes __ / No __   2. Yes __ / No __   3. Yes __ / No __   4. Yes __ / No __

Decision: _____   Benefit: _____

Topic 2: _____   Rationales: _____

Suggestions:

1. _____   2. _____

_____   _____

3. _____   4. _____

_____   _____

Vote   1. Yes __ / No __   2. Yes __ / No __   3. Yes __ / No __   4. Yes __ / No __

Decision: _____   Benefit: _____

Family Meetings should create a tone of peace, communication, order, justice, freedom, and safety

TOPICS TO BE DISCUSSED AT THE NEXT MEETING

	Date / Name	Topic

ADDITIONAL NOTES

FAMILY MEETING

Creating Healthy Family Communication

Time Began: _____ Ended: _____ Led by: _____ Date: _____

Announcements: _____

_____

_____

Topic Examples: Family activities, family problems, standards, motivational systems, and consequences.

Rules: No pointing fingers, name calling, etc. Topics should never target a person. Those issues can be discussed in mentor meetings. When discussing rationales, decisions and benefits, keep top-of-mind: Fair, effective, love and concern, pleasant atmosphere.

Topic 1: _____ Rationales: _____

Suggestions:

1. _____ 2. _____

_____ _____

3. _____ 4. _____

_____ _____

Vote   1. Yes __ / No __   2. Yes __ / No __   3. Yes __ / No __   4. Yes __ / No __

Decision: _____ Benefit: _____

Topic 2: _____ Rationales: _____

Suggestions:

1. _____ 2. _____

_____ _____

3. _____ 4. _____

_____ _____

Vote   1. Yes __ / No __   2. Yes __ / No __   3. Yes __ / No __   4. Yes __ / No __

Decision: _____ Benefit: _____

Family Meetings should create a tone of peace, communication, order, justice, freedom, and safety

TOPICS TO BE DISCUSSED AT THE NEXT MEETING

	Date / Name	Topic

ADDITIONAL NOTES

FAMILY MEETING
Creating Healthy Family Communication

Time Began: _____ Ended: _____ Led by: _____ Date: _____

Announcements: _____

_____

_____

Topic Examples: Family activities, family problems, standards, motivational systems, and consequences.

Rules: No pointing fingers, name calling, etc. Topics should never target a person. Those issues can be discussed in mentor meetings. When discussing rationales, decisions and benefits, keep top-of-mind: Fair, effective, love and concern, pleasant atmosphere.

Topic 1: _____ Rationales: _____

Suggestions:

1. _____   2. _____

3. _____   4. _____

Vote   1. Yes __ / No __   2. Yes __ / No __   3. Yes __ / No __   4. Yes __ / No __

Decision: _____   Benefit: _____

Topic 2: _____ Rationales: _____

Suggestions:

1. _____   2. _____

3. _____   4. _____

Vote   1. Yes __ / No __   2. Yes __ / No __   3. Yes __ / No __   4. Yes __ / No __

Decision: _____   Benefit: _____

Family Meetings should create a tone of peace, communication, order, justice, freedom, and safety

TOPICS TO BE DISCUSSED AT THE NEXT MEETING

	Date / Name	Topic

ADDITIONAL NOTES

FAMILY MEETING

Creating Healthy Family Communication

Time Began: _____ Ended: _____ Led by: _____ Date: _____

Announcements: _____

_____

_____

Topic Examples: Family activities, family problems, standards, motivational systems, and consequences.

Rules: No pointing fingers, name calling, etc. Topics should never target a person. Those issues can be discussed in mentor meetings. When discussing rationales, decisions and benefits, keep top-of-mind: Fair, effective, love and concern, pleasant atmosphere.

Topic 1: _____ Rationales: _____

Suggestions:

1. _____ 2. _____

3. _____ 4. _____

Vote   1. Yes __ / No __   2. Yes __ / No __   3. Yes __ / No __   4. Yes __ / No __

Decision: _____ Benefit: _____

Topic 2: _____ Rationales: _____

Suggestions:

1. _____ 2. _____

3. _____ 4. _____

Vote   1. Yes __ / No __   2. Yes __ / No __   3. Yes __ / No __   4. Yes __ / No __

Decision: _____ Benefit: _____

Family Meetings should create a tone of peace, communication, order, justice, freedom, and safety

TOPICS TO BE DISCUSSED AT THE NEXT MEETING

	Date / Name	Topic

ADDITIONAL NOTES

FAMILY MEETING

Creating Healthy Family Communication

Time Began: _____ Ended: _____ Led by: _____ Date: _____

Announcements: _____

_____

_____

Topic Examples: Family activities, family problems, standards, motivational systems, and consequences.

Rules: No pointing fingers, name calling, etc. Topics should never target a person. Those issues can be discussed in mentor meetings. When discussing rationales, decisions and benefits, keep top-of-mind: Fair, effective, love and concern, pleasant atmosphere.

Topic 1: _____ Rationales: _____

Suggestions:

1. _____ 2. _____

3. _____ 4. _____

Vote   1. Yes __ / No __   2. Yes __ / No __   3. Yes __ / No __   4. Yes __ / No __

Decision: _____ Benefit: _____

Topic 2: _____ Rationales: _____

Suggestions:

1. _____ 2. _____

3. _____ 4. _____

Vote   1. Yes __ / No __   2. Yes __ / No __   3. Yes __ / No __   4. Yes __ / No __

Decision: _____ Benefit: _____

Family Meetings should create a tone of peace, communication, order, justice, freedom, and safety

TOPICS TO BE DISCUSSED AT THE NEXT MEETING

	Date / Name	Topic

ADDITIONAL NOTES

FAMILY MEETING

Creating Healthy Family Communication

Time Began: _____ Ended: _____ Led by: _____ Date: _____

Announcements: _____

_____

_____

Topic Examples: Family activities, family problems, standards, motivational systems, and consequences.

Rules: No pointing fingers, name calling, etc. Topics should never target a person. Those issues can be discussed in mentor meetings. When discussing rationales, decisions and benefits, keep top-of-mind: Fair, effective, love and concern, pleasant atmosphere.

Topic 1: _____ Rationales: _____

Suggestions:

1. _____ 2. _____

_____ _____

3. _____ 4. _____

_____ _____

Vote   1. Yes __ / No __   2. Yes __ / No __   3. Yes __ / No __   4. Yes __ / No __

Decision: _____ Benefit: _____

Topic 2: _____ Rationales: _____

Suggestions:

1. _____ 2. _____

_____ _____

3. _____ 4. _____

_____ _____

Vote   1. Yes __ / No __   2. Yes __ / No __   3. Yes __ / No __   4. Yes __ / No __

Decision: _____ Benefit: _____

Family Meetings should create a tone of peace, communication, order, justice, freedom, and safety

TOPICS TO BE DISCUSSED AT THE NEXT MEETING

	Date / Name	Topic

ADDITIONAL NOTES

FAMILY MEETING
Creating Healthy Family Communication

Time Began: _____ Ended: _____ Led by: _____ Date: _____

Announcements: _____

_____

_____

Topic Examples: Family activities, family problems, standards, motivational systems, and consequences.

Rules: No pointing fingers, name calling, etc. Topics should never target a person. Those issues can be discussed in mentor meetings. When discussing rationales, decisions and benefits, keep top-of-mind: Fair, effective, love and concern, pleasant atmosphere.

Topic 1: _____ Rationales: _____

Suggestions:

1. _____   2. _____

_____   _____

3. _____   4. _____

_____   _____

Vote   1. Yes __ / No __   2. Yes __ / No __   3. Yes __ / No __   4. Yes __ / No __

Decision: _____ Benefit: _____

Topic 2: _____ Rationales: _____

Suggestions:

1. _____   2. _____

_____   _____

3. _____   4. _____

_____   _____

Vote   1. Yes __ / No __   2. Yes __ / No __   3. Yes __ / No __   4. Yes __ / No __

Decision: _____ Benefit: _____

Family Meetings should create a tone of peace, communication, order, justice, freedom, and safety

TOPICS TO BE DISCUSSED AT THE NEXT MEETING

	Date / Name	Topic

ADDITIONAL NOTES

FAMILY MEETING

Creating Healthy Family Communication

Time Began: _____ Ended: _____ Led by: _____ Date: _____

Announcements: _____

_____

_____

Topic Examples: Family activities, family problems, standards, motivational systems, and consequences.

Rules: No pointing fingers, name calling, etc. Topics should never target a person. Those issues can be discussed in mentor meetings. When discussing rationales, decisions and benefits, keep top-of-mind: Fair, effective, love and concern, pleasant atmosphere.

Topic 1: _____ Rationales: _____

Suggestions:

1. _____ 2. _____

_____ _____

3. _____ 4. _____

_____ _____

Vote   1. Yes __ / No __   2. Yes __ / No __   3. Yes __ / No __   4. Yes __ / No __

Decision: _____ Benefit: _____

Topic 2: _____ Rationales: _____

Suggestions:

1. _____ 2. _____

_____ _____

3. _____ 4. _____

_____ _____

Vote   1. Yes __ / No __   2. Yes __ / No __   3. Yes __ / No __   4. Yes __ / No __

Decision: _____ Benefit: _____

Family Meetings should create a tone of peace, communication, order, justice, freedom, and safety

TOPICS TO BE DISCUSSED AT THE NEXT MEETING

	Date / Name	Topic

ADDITIONAL NOTES

FAMILY MEETING
Creating Healthy Family Communication

Time Began: _____ Ended: _____ Led by: _____ Date: _____

Announcements: _____

_____

_____

Topic Examples: Family activities, family problems, standards, motivational systems, and consequences.

Rules: No pointing fingers, name calling, etc. Topics should never target a person. Those issues can be discussed in mentor meetings. When discussing rationales, decisions and benefits, keep top-of-mind: Fair, effective, love and concern, pleasant atmosphere.

Topic 1: _____ Rationales: _____

Suggestions:

1. _____ 2. _____

_____ _____

3. _____ 4. _____

_____ _____

Vote   1. Yes __ / No __   2. Yes __ / No __   3. Yes __ / No __   4. Yes __ / No __

Decision: _____ Benefit: _____

Topic 2: _____ Rationales: _____

Suggestions:

1. _____ 2. _____

_____ _____

3. _____ 4. _____

_____ _____

Vote   1. Yes __ / No __   2. Yes __ / No __   3. Yes __ / No __   4. Yes __ / No __

Decision: _____ Benefit: _____

Family Meetings should create a tone of peace, communication, order, justice, freedom, and safety

TOPICS TO BE DISCUSSED AT THE NEXT MEETING

	Date / Name	Topic

ADDITIONAL NOTES

FAMILY MEETING
Creating Healthy Family Communication

Time Began: _____ Ended: _____ Led by: _____ Date: _____

Announcements: _____

_____

_____

Topic Examples: Family activities, family problems, standards, motivational systems, and consequences.

Rules: No pointing fingers, name calling, etc. Topics should never target a person. Those issues can be discussed in mentor meetings. When discussing rationales, decisions and benefits, keep top-of-mind: Fair, effective, love and concern, pleasant atmosphere.

Topic 1: _____ Rationales: _____

Suggestions:

1. _____ 2. _____

3. _____ 4. _____

Vote   1. Yes __ / No __   2. Yes __ / No __   3. Yes __ / No __   4. Yes __ / No __

Decision: _____ Benefit: _____

Topic 2: _____ Rationales: _____

Suggestions:

1. _____ 2. _____

3. _____ 4. _____

Vote   1. Yes __ / No __   2. Yes __ / No __   3. Yes __ / No __   4. Yes __ / No __

Decision: _____ Benefit: _____

Family Meetings should create a tone of peace, communication, order, justice, freedom, and safety

TOPICS TO BE DISCUSSED AT THE NEXT MEETING

	Date / Name	Topic

ADDITIONAL NOTES

FAMILY MEETING
Creating Healthy Family Communication

Time Began: _____ Ended: _____ Led by: _____ Date: _____

Announcements: _____

_____

_____

Topic Examples: Family activities, family problems, standards, motivational systems, and consequences.

Rules: No pointing fingers, name calling, etc. Topics should never target a person. Those issues can be discussed in mentor meetings. When discussing rationales, decisions and benefits, keep top-of-mind: Fair, effective, love and concern, pleasant atmosphere.

Topic 1: _____ Rationales: _____

Suggestions:

1. _____   2. _____

   _____   _____

3. _____   4. _____

   _____   _____

Vote   1. Yes __ / No __   2. Yes __ / No __   3. Yes __ / No __   4. Yes __ / No __

Decision: _____ Benefit: _____

Topic 2: _____ Rationales: _____

Suggestions:

1. _____   2. _____

   _____   _____

3. _____   4. _____

   _____   _____

Vote   1. Yes __ / No __   2. Yes __ / No __   3. Yes __ / No __   4. Yes __ / No __

Decision: _____ Benefit: _____

Family Meetings should create a tone of peace, communication, order, justice, freedom, and safety

TOPICS TO BE DISCUSSED AT THE NEXT MEETING

	Date / Name	Topic

ADDITIONAL NOTES

FAMILY MEETING
Creating Healthy Family Communication

Time Began: _____ Ended: _____ Led by: _____ Date: _____

Announcements: _____

_____

_____

Topic Examples: Family activities, family problems, standards, motivational systems, and consequences.

Rules: No pointing fingers, name calling, etc. Topics should never target a person. Those issues can be discussed in mentor meetings. When discussing rationales, decisions and benefits, keep top-of-mind: Fair, effective, love and concern, pleasant atmosphere.

Topic 1: _____ Rationales: _____

Suggestions:

1. _____   2. _____

_____   _____

3. _____   4. _____

_____   _____

Vote   1. Yes __ / No __   2. Yes __ / No __   3. Yes __ / No __   4. Yes __ / No __

Decision: _____ Benefit: _____

Topic 2: _____ Rationales: _____

Suggestions:

1. _____   2. _____

_____   _____

3. _____   4. _____

_____   _____

Vote   1. Yes __ / No __   2. Yes __ / No __   3. Yes __ / No __   4. Yes __ / No __

Decision: _____ Benefit: _____

Family Meetings should create a tone of peace, communication, order, justice, freedom, and safety

TOPICS TO BE DISCUSSED AT THE NEXT MEETING

	Date / Name	Topic

ADDITIONAL NOTES

FAMILY MEETING
Creating Healthy Family Communication

Time Began: _____ Ended: _____ Led by: _____ Date: _____

Announcements: _____

_____

_____

Topic Examples: Family activities, family problems, standards, motivational systems, and consequences.

Rules: No pointing fingers, name calling, etc. Topics should never target a person. Those issues can be discussed in mentor meetings. When discussing rationales, decisions and benefits, keep top-of-mind: Fair, effective, love and concern, pleasant atmosphere.

Topic 1: _____ Rationales: _____

Suggestions:

1. _____ 2. _____

_____ _____

3. _____ 4. _____

_____ _____

Vote   1. Yes __ / No __   2. Yes __ / No __   3. Yes __ / No __   4. Yes __ / No __

Decision: _____ Benefit: _____

Topic 2: _____ Rationales: _____

Suggestions:

1. _____ 2. _____

_____ _____

3. _____ 4. _____

_____ _____

Vote   1. Yes __ / No __   2. Yes __ / No __   3. Yes __ / No __   4. Yes __ / No __

Decision: _____ Benefit: _____

Family Meetings should create a tone of peace, communication, order, justice, freedom, and safety

TOPICS TO BE DISCUSSED AT THE NEXT MEETING

	Date / Name	Topic

ADDITIONAL NOTES

FAMILY MEETING
Creating Healthy Family Communication

Time Began: _____ Ended: _____ Led by: _____ Date: _____

Announcements: _____

_____

_____

Topic Examples: Family activities, family problems, standards, motivational systems, and consequences.

Rules: No pointing fingers, name calling, etc. Topics should never target a person. Those issues can be discussed in mentor meetings. When discussing rationales, decisions and benefits, keep top-of-mind: Fair, effective, love and concern, pleasant atmosphere.

Topic 1: _____ Rationales: _____

Suggestions:

1. _____ 2. _____

_____ _____

3. _____ 4. _____

_____ _____

Vote   1. Yes __ / No __   2. Yes __ / No __   3. Yes __ / No __   4. Yes __ / No __

Decision: _____ Benefit: _____

Topic 2: _____ Rationales: _____

Suggestions:

1. _____ 2. _____

_____ _____

3. _____ 4. _____

_____ _____

Vote   1. Yes __ / No __   2. Yes __ / No __   3. Yes __ / No __   4. Yes __ / No __

Decision: _____ Benefit: _____

Family Meetings should create a tone of peace, communication, order, justice, freedom, and safety

TOPICS TO BE DISCUSSED AT THE NEXT MEETING

	Date / Name	Topic

ADDITIONAL NOTES

FAMILY MEETING

Creating Healthy Family Communication

Time Began: _____ Ended: _____ Led by: _____ Date: _____

Announcements: _____

_____

_____

Topic Examples: Family activities, family problems, standards, motivational systems, and consequences.

Rules: No pointing fingers, name calling, etc. Topics should never target a person. Those issues can be discussed in mentor meetings. When discussing rationales, decisions and benefits, keep top-of-mind: Fair, effective, love and concern, pleasant atmosphere.

Topic 1: _____ Rationales: _____

Suggestions:

1. _____ 2. _____

_____ _____

3. _____ 4. _____

_____ _____

Vote　　　　1. Yes __ / No __　　2. Yes __ / No __　　3. Yes __ / No __　　4. Yes __ / No __

Decision: _____ Benefit: _____

Topic 2: _____ Rationales: _____

Suggestions:

1. _____ 2. _____

_____ _____

3. _____ 4. _____

_____ _____

Vote　　　　1. Yes __ / No __　　2. Yes __ / No __　　3. Yes __ / No __　　4. Yes __ / No __

Decision: _____ Benefit: _____

Family Meetings should create a tone of peace, communication, order, justice, freedom, and safety

TOPICS TO BE DISCUSSED AT THE NEXT MEETING

	Date / Name	Topic

ADDITIONAL NOTES

FAMILY MEETING

Creating Healthy Family Communication

Time Began: _____ Ended: _____ Led by: _____ Date: _____

Announcements: _____

_____

_____

Topic Examples: Family activities, family problems, standards, motivational systems, and consequences.

Rules: No pointing fingers, name calling, etc. Topics should never target a person. Those issues can be discussed in mentor meetings. When discussing rationales, decisions and benefits, keep top-of-mind: Fair, effective, love and concern, pleasant atmosphere.

Topic 1: _____ Rationales: _____

Suggestions:

1. _____ 2. _____

3. _____ 4. _____

Vote   1. Yes __ / No __   2. Yes __ / No __   3. Yes __ / No __   4. Yes __ / No __

Decision: _____ Benefit: _____

Topic 2: _____ Rationales: _____

Suggestions:

1. _____ 2. _____

3. _____ 4. _____

Vote   1. Yes __ / No __   2. Yes __ / No __   3. Yes __ / No __   4. Yes __ / No __

Decision: _____ Benefit: _____

Family Meetings should create a tone of peace, communication, order, justice, freedom, and safety

TOPICS TO BE DISCUSSED AT THE NEXT MEETING

	Date / Name	Topic

ADDITIONAL NOTES

_____

_____

_____

_____

_____

_____

_____

_____

_____

_____

FAMILY MEETING
Creating Healthy Family Communication

Time Began: _____ Ended: _____ Led by: _____ Date: _____

Announcements: _____

_____

_____

Topic Examples: Family activities, family problems, standards, motivational systems, and consequences.

Rules: No pointing fingers, name calling, etc. Topics should never target a person. Those issues can be discussed in mentor meetings. When discussing rationales, decisions and benefits, keep top-of-mind: Fair, effective, love and concern, pleasant atmosphere.

Topic 1: _____ Rationales: _____

Suggestions:

1. _____ 2. _____

_____ _____

3. _____ 4. _____

_____ _____

Vote   1. Yes __ / No __   2. Yes __ / No __   3. Yes __ / No __   4. Yes __ / No __

Decision: _____ Benefit: _____

Topic 2: _____ Rationales: _____

Suggestions:

1. _____ 2. _____

_____ _____

3. _____ 4. _____

_____ _____

Vote   1. Yes __ / No __   2. Yes __ / No __   3. Yes __ / No __   4. Yes __ / No __

Decision: _____ Benefit: _____

Family Meetings should create a tone of peace, communication, order, justice, freedom, and safety

TOPICS TO BE DISCUSSED AT THE NEXT MEETING

	Date / Name	Topic

ADDITIONAL NOTES

FAMILY MEETING

Creating Healthy Family Communication

Time Began: _____ Ended: _____ Led by: _____ Date: _____

Announcements: _____

_____

_____

Topic Examples: Family activities, family problems, standards, motivational systems, and consequences.

Rules: No pointing fingers, name calling, etc. Topics should never target a person. Those issues can be discussed in mentor meetings. When discussing rationales, decisions and benefits, keep top-of-mind: Fair, effective, love and concern, pleasant atmosphere.

Topic 1: _____ Rationales: _____

Suggestions:

1. _____ 2. _____

_____ _____

3. _____ 4. _____

_____ _____

Vote   1. Yes __ / No __   2. Yes __ / No __   3. Yes __ / No __   4. Yes __ / No __

Decision: _____ Benefit: _____

Topic 2: _____ Rationales: _____

Suggestions:

1. _____ 2. _____

_____ _____

3. _____ 4. _____

_____ _____

Vote   1. Yes __ / No __   2. Yes __ / No __   3. Yes __ / No __   4. Yes __ / No __

Decision: _____ Benefit: _____

Family Meetings should create a tone of peace, communication, order, justice, freedom, and safety

TOPICS TO BE DISCUSSED AT THE NEXT MEETING

	Date / Name	Topic

ADDITIONAL NOTES

FAMILY MEETING
Creating Healthy Family Communication

Time Began: _____ Ended: _____ Led by: _____ Date: _____

Announcements: _____

_____

_____

Topic Examples: Family activities, family problems, standards, motivational systems, and consequences.

Rules: No pointing fingers, name calling, etc. Topics should never target a person. Those issues can be discussed in mentor meetings. When discussing rationales, decisions and benefits, keep top-of-mind: Fair, effective, love and concern, pleasant atmosphere.

Topic 1: _____ Rationales: _____

Suggestions:

1. _____ 2. _____

_____ _____

3. _____ 4. _____

_____ _____

Vote   1. Yes __ / No __   2. Yes __ / No __   3. Yes __ / No __   4. Yes __ / No __

Decision: _____ Benefit: _____

Topic 2: _____ Rationales: _____

Suggestions:

1. _____ 2. _____

_____ _____

3. _____ 4. _____

_____ _____

Vote   1. Yes __ / No __   2. Yes __ / No __   3. Yes __ / No __   4. Yes __ / No __

Decision: _____ Benefit: _____

Family Meetings should create a tone of peace, communication, order, justice, freedom, and safety

TOPICS TO BE DISCUSSED AT THE NEXT MEETING

	Date / Name	Topic

ADDITIONAL NOTES

FAMILY MEETING
Creating Healthy Family Communication

Time Began: _____ Ended: _____ Led by: _____ Date: _____

Announcements: _____

_____

_____

Topic Examples: Family activities, family problems, standards, motivational systems, and consequences.

Rules: No pointing fingers, name calling, etc. Topics should never target a person. Those issues can be discussed in mentor meetings. When discussing rationales, decisions and benefits, keep top-of-mind: Fair, effective, love and concern, pleasant atmosphere.

Topic 1: _____ Rationales: _____

Suggestions:

1. _____ 2. _____

3. _____ 4. _____

Vote   1. Yes __ / No __   2. Yes __ / No __   3. Yes __ / No __   4. Yes __ / No __

Decision: _____ Benefit: _____

Topic 2: _____ Rationales: _____

Suggestions:

1. _____ 2. _____

3. _____ 4. _____

Vote   1. Yes __ / No __   2. Yes __ / No __   3. Yes __ / No __   4. Yes __ / No __

Decision: _____ Benefit: _____

Family Meetings should create a tone of peace, communication, order, justice, freedom, and safety

TOPICS TO BE DISCUSSED AT THE NEXT MEETING

	Date / Name	Topic

ADDITIONAL NOTES

FAMILY MEETING

Creating Healthy Family Communication

Time Began: _____ Ended: _____ Led by: _____ Date: _____

Announcements: _____

_____

_____

Topic Examples: Family activities, family problems, standards, motivational systems, and consequences.

Rules: No pointing fingers, name calling, etc. Topics should never target a person. Those issues can be discussed in mentor meetings. When discussing rationales, decisions and benefits, keep top-of-mind: Fair, effective, love and concern, pleasant atmosphere.

Topic 1: _____   Rationales: _____

Suggestions:

1. _____   2. _____

_____   _____

3. _____   4. _____

_____   _____

Vote   1. Yes __ / No __   2. Yes __ / No __   3. Yes __ / No __   4. Yes __ / No __

Decision: _____   Benefit: _____

Topic 2: _____   Rationales: _____

Suggestions:

1. _____   2. _____

_____   _____

3. _____   4. _____

_____   _____

Vote   1. Yes __ / No __   2. Yes __ / No __   3. Yes __ / No __   4. Yes __ / No __

Decision: _____   Benefit: _____

Family Meetings should create a tone of peace, communication, order, justice, freedom, and safety

TOPICS TO BE DISCUSSED AT THE NEXT MEETING

	Date / Name	Topic

ADDITIONAL NOTES

FAMILY MEETING
Creating Healthy Family Communication

Time Began: _____ Ended: _____ Led by: _____ Date: _____

Announcements: _____

_____

_____

Topic Examples: Family activities, family problems, standards, motivational systems, and consequences.

Rules: No pointing fingers, name calling, etc. Topics should never target a person. Those issues can be discussed in mentor meetings. When discussing rationales, decisions and benefits, keep top-of-mind: Fair, effective, love and concern, pleasant atmosphere.

Topic 1: _____ Rationales: _____

Suggestions:

1. _____ 2. _____

_____ _____

3. _____ 4. _____

_____ _____

Vote   1. Yes __ / No __   2. Yes __ / No __   3. Yes __ / No __   4. Yes __ / No __

Decision: _____ Benefit: _____

Topic 2: _____ Rationales: _____

Suggestions:

1. _____ 2. _____

_____ _____

3. _____ 4. _____

_____ _____

Vote   1. Yes __ / No __   2. Yes __ / No __   3. Yes __ / No __   4. Yes __ / No __

Decision: _____ Benefit: _____

Family Meetings should create a tone of peace, communication, order, justice, freedom, and safety

TOPICS TO BE DISCUSSED AT THE NEXT MEETING

	Date / Name	Topic

ADDITIONAL NOTES

FAMILY MEETING

Creating Healthy Family Communication

Time Began: _____ Ended: _____ Led by: _____ Date: _____

Announcements: _____

_____

_____

Topic Examples: Family activities, family problems, standards, motivational systems, and consequences.

Rules: No pointing fingers, name calling, etc. Topics should never target a person. Those issues can be discussed in mentor meetings. When discussing rationales, decisions and benefits, keep top-of-mind: Fair, effective, love and concern, pleasant atmosphere.

Topic 1: _____ Rationales: _____

Suggestions:

1. _____ 2. _____

_____ _____

3. _____ 4. _____

_____ _____

Vote   1. Yes __ / No __   2. Yes __ / No __   3. Yes __ / No __   4. Yes __ / No __

Decision: _____ Benefit: _____

Topic 2: _____ Rationales: _____

Suggestions:

1. _____ 2. _____

_____ _____

3. _____ 4. _____

_____ _____

Vote   1. Yes __ / No __   2. Yes __ / No __   3. Yes __ / No __   4. Yes __ / No __

Decision: _____ Benefit: _____

Family Meetings should create a tone of peace, communication, order, justice, freedom, and safety

TOPICS TO BE DISCUSSED AT THE NEXT MEETING

	Date / Name	Topic

ADDITIONAL NOTES

FAMILY MEETING
Creating Healthy Family Communication

Time Began: _____ Ended: _____ Led by: _____ Date: _____

Announcements: _____

_____

_____

Topic Examples: Family activities, family problems, standards, motivational systems, and consequences.

Rules: No pointing fingers, name calling, etc. Topics should never target a person. Those issues can be discussed in mentor meetings. When discussing rationales, decisions and benefits, keep top-of-mind: Fair, effective, love and concern, pleasant atmosphere.

Topic 1: _____ Rationales: _____

Suggestions:

1. _____   2. _____

   _____   _____

3. _____   4. _____

   _____   _____

Vote   1. Yes __ / No __   2. Yes __ / No __   3. Yes __ / No __   4. Yes __ / No __

Decision: _____ Benefit: _____

Topic 2: _____ Rationales: _____

Suggestions:

1. _____   2. _____

   _____   _____

3. _____   4. _____

   _____   _____

Vote   1. Yes __ / No __   2. Yes __ / No __   3. Yes __ / No __   4. Yes __ / No __

Decision: _____ Benefit: _____

Family Meetings should create a tone of peace, communication, order, justice, freedom, and safety

TOPICS TO BE DISCUSSED AT THE NEXT MEETING

	Date / Name	Topic

ADDITIONAL NOTES

_____

_____

_____

_____

_____

_____

_____

_____

_____

FAMILY MEETING

Creating Healthy Family Communication

Time Began: _____ Ended: _____ Led by: _____ Date: _____

Announcements: _____

_____

_____

Topic Examples: Family activities, family problems, standards, motivational systems, and consequences.

Rules: No pointing fingers, name calling, etc. Topics should never target a person. Those issues can be discussed in mentor meetings. When discussing rationales, decisions and benefits, keep top-of-mind: Fair, effective, love and concern, pleasant atmosphere.

Topic 1: _____   Rationales: _____

Suggestions:

1. _____   2. _____

_____   _____

3. _____   4. _____

_____   _____

Vote   1. Yes __ / No __   2. Yes __ / No __   3. Yes __ / No __   4. Yes __ / No __

Decision: _____   Benefit: _____

Topic 2: _____   Rationales: _____

Suggestions:

1. _____   2. _____

_____   _____

3. _____   4. _____

_____   _____

Vote   1. Yes __ / No __   2. Yes __ / No __   3. Yes __ / No __   4. Yes __ / No __

Decision: _____   Benefit: _____

Family Meetings should create a tone of peace, communication, order, justice, freedom, and safety

TOPICS TO BE DISCUSSED AT THE NEXT MEETING

	Date / Name	Topic

ADDITIONAL NOTES

FAMILY MEETING

Creating Healthy Family Communication

Time Began: _____ Ended: _____ Led by: _____ Date: _____

Announcements: _____

_____

_____

Topic Examples: Family activities, family problems, standards, motivational systems, and consequences.

Rules: No pointing fingers, name calling, etc. Topics should never target a person. Those issues can be discussed in mentor meetings. When discussing rationales, decisions and benefits, keep top-of-mind: Fair, effective, love and concern, pleasant atmosphere.

Topic 1: _____ Rationales: _____

Suggestions:

1. _____ 2. _____

_____ _____

3. _____ 4. _____

_____ _____

Vote   1. Yes __ / No __   2. Yes __ / No __   3. Yes __ / No __   4. Yes __ / No __

Decision: _____ Benefit: _____

Topic 2: _____ Rationales: _____

Suggestions:

1. _____ 2. _____

_____ _____

3. _____ 4. _____

_____ _____

Vote   1. Yes __ / No __   2. Yes __ / No __   3. Yes __ / No __   4. Yes __ / No __

Decision: _____ Benefit: _____

Family Meetings should create a tone of peace, communication, order, justice, freedom, and safety

TOPICS TO BE DISCUSSED AT THE NEXT MEETING

	Date / Name	Topic

ADDITIONAL NOTES

_____

_____

_____

_____

_____

_____

_____

_____

_____

_____

FAMILY MEETING
Creating Healthy Family Communication

Time Began: _____ Ended: _____ Led by: _____ Date: _____

Announcements: _____

_____

_____

Topic Examples: Family activities, family problems, standards, motivational systems, and consequences.

Rules: No pointing fingers, name calling, etc. Topics should never target a person. Those issues can be discussed in mentor meetings. When discussing rationales, decisions and benefits, keep top-of-mind: Fair, effective, love and concern, pleasant atmosphere.

Topic 1: _____ Rationales: _____

Suggestions:

1. _____   2. _____

_____   _____

3. _____   4. _____

_____   _____

Vote   1. Yes __ / No __   2. Yes __ / No __   3. Yes __ / No __   4. Yes __ / No __

Decision: _____   Benefit: _____

Topic 2: _____ Rationales: _____

Suggestions:

1. _____   2. _____

_____   _____

3. _____   4. _____

_____   _____

Vote   1. Yes __ / No __   2. Yes __ / No __   3. Yes __ / No __   4. Yes __ / No __

Decision: _____   Benefit: _____

Family Meetings should create a tone of peace, communication, order, justice, freedom, and safety

TOPICS TO BE DISCUSSED AT THE NEXT MEETING

	Date / Name	Topic

ADDITIONAL NOTES

_____

_____

_____

_____

_____

_____

_____

_____

_____

FAMILY MEETING

Creating Healthy Family Communication

Time Began: _____ Ended: _____ Led by: _____ Date: _____

Announcements: _____

_____

_____

Topic Examples: Family activities, family problems, standards, motivational systems, and consequences.

Rules: No pointing fingers, name calling, etc. Topics should never target a person. Those issues can be discussed in mentor meetings. When discussing rationales, decisions and benefits, keep top-of-mind: Fair, effective, love and concern, pleasant atmosphere.

Topic 1: _____ Rationales: _____

Suggestions:

1. _____ 2. _____

_____ _____

3. _____ 4. _____

_____ _____

Vote   1. Yes __ / No __   2. Yes __ / No __   3. Yes __ / No __   4. Yes __ / No __

Decision: _____ Benefit: _____

Topic 2: _____ Rationales: _____

Suggestions:

1. _____ 2. _____

_____ _____

3. _____ 4. _____

_____ _____

Vote   1. Yes __ / No __   2. Yes __ / No __   3. Yes __ / No __   4. Yes __ / No __

Decision: _____ Benefit: _____

Family Meetings should create a tone of peace, communication, order, justice, freedom, and safety

TOPICS TO BE DISCUSSED AT THE NEXT MEETING

	Date / Name	Topic

ADDITIONAL NOTES

_____

_____

_____

_____

_____

_____

_____

_____

_____

FAMILY MEETING

Creating Healthy Family Communication

Time Began: _____ Ended: _____ Led by: _____ Date: _____

Announcements: _____

_____

_____

Topic Examples: Family activities, family problems, standards, motivational systems, and consequences.

Rules: No pointing fingers, name calling, etc. Topics should never target a person. Those issues can be discussed in mentor meetings. When discussing rationales, decisions and benefits, keep top-of-mind: Fair, effective, love and concern, pleasant atmosphere.

Topic 1: _____ Rationales: _____

Suggestions:

1. _____ 2. _____

_____ _____

3. _____ 4. _____

_____ _____

Vote   1. Yes __ / No __   2. Yes __ / No __   3. Yes __ / No __   4. Yes __ / No __

Decision: _____ Benefit: _____

Topic 2: _____ Rationales: _____

Suggestions:

1. _____ 2. _____

_____ _____

3. _____ 4. _____

_____ _____

Vote   1. Yes __ / No __   2. Yes __ / No __   3. Yes __ / No __   4. Yes __ / No __

Decision: _____ Benefit: _____

Family Meetings should create a tone of peace, communication, order, justice, freedom, and safety

TOPICS TO BE DISCUSSED AT THE NEXT MEETING

	Date / Name	Topic

ADDITIONAL NOTES

FAMILY MEETING
Creating Healthy Family Communication

Time Began: _____ Ended: _____ Led by: _____ Date: _____

Announcements: _____

_____

_____

Topic Examples: Family activities, family problems, standards, motivational systems, and consequences.

Rules: No pointing fingers, name calling, etc. Topics should never target a person. Those issues can be discussed in mentor meetings. When discussing rationales, decisions and benefits, keep top-of-mind: Fair, effective, love and concern, pleasant atmosphere.

Topic 1: _____ Rationales: _____

Suggestions:

1. _____ 2. _____

_____ _____

3. _____ 4. _____

_____ _____

Vote   1. Yes __ / No __   2. Yes __ / No __   3. Yes __ / No __   4. Yes __ / No __

Decision: _____ Benefit: _____

Topic 2: _____ Rationales: _____

Suggestions:

1. _____ 2. _____

_____ _____

3. _____ 4. _____

_____ _____

Vote   1. Yes __ / No __   2. Yes __ / No __   3. Yes __ / No __   4. Yes __ / No __

Decision: _____ Benefit: _____

Family Meetings should create a tone of peace, communication, order, justice, freedom, and safety

TOPICS TO BE DISCUSSED AT THE NEXT MEETING

	Date / Name	Topic

ADDITIONAL NOTES

FAMILY MEETING

Creating Healthy Family Communication

Time Began: _____ Ended: _____ Led by: _____ Date: _____

Announcements: _____

_____

_____

Topic Examples: Family activities, family problems, standards, motivational systems, and consequences.

Rules: No pointing fingers, name calling, etc. Topics should never target a person. Those issues can be discussed in mentor meetings. When discussing rationales, decisions and benefits, keep top-of-mind: Fair, effective, love and concern, pleasant atmosphere.

Topic 1: _____ Rationales: _____

Suggestions:

1. _____   2. _____

_____   _____

3. _____   4. _____

_____   _____

Vote   1. Yes __ / No __   2. Yes __ / No __   3. Yes __ / No __   4. Yes __ / No __

Decision: _____ Benefit: _____

Topic 2: _____ Rationales: _____

Suggestions:

1. _____   2. _____

_____   _____

3. _____   4. _____

_____   _____

Vote   1. Yes __ / No __   2. Yes __ / No __   3. Yes __ / No __   4. Yes __ / No __

Decision: _____ Benefit: _____

Family Meetings should create a tone of peace, communication, order, justice, freedom, and safety

TOPICS TO BE DISCUSSED AT THE NEXT MEETING

	Date / Name	Topic

ADDITIONAL NOTES

FAMILY MEETING
Creating Healthy Family Communication

Time Began: _____ Ended: _____ Led by: _____ Date: _____

Announcements: _____

_____

_____

Topic Examples: Family activities, family problems, standards, motivational systems, and consequences.

Rules: No pointing fingers, name calling, etc. Topics should never target a person. Those issues can be discussed in mentor meetings. When discussing rationales, decisions and benefits, keep top-of-mind: Fair, effective, love and concern, pleasant atmosphere.

Topic 1: _____ Rationales: _____

Suggestions:

1. _____ 2. _____

_____ _____

3. _____ 4. _____

_____ _____

Vote   1. Yes __ / No __   2. Yes __ / No __   3. Yes __ / No __   4. Yes __ / No __

Decision: _____ Benefit: _____

Topic 2: _____ Rationales: _____

Suggestions:

1. _____ 2. _____

_____ _____

3. _____ 4. _____

_____ _____

Vote   1. Yes __ / No __   2. Yes __ / No __   3. Yes __ / No __   4. Yes __ / No __

Decision: _____ Benefit: _____

Family Meetings should create a tone of peace, communication, order, justice, freedom, and safety

TOPICS TO BE DISCUSSED AT THE NEXT MEETING

	Date / Name	Topic

ADDITIONAL NOTES

FAMILY MEETING
Creating Healthy Family Communication

Time Began: _____ Ended: _____ Led by: _____ Date: _____

Announcements: _____

_____

_____

Topic Examples: Family activities, family problems, standards, motivational systems, and consequences.

Rules: No pointing fingers, name calling, etc. Topics should never target a person. Those issues can be discussed in mentor meetings. When discussing rationales, decisions and benefits, keep top-of-mind: Fair, effective, love and concern, pleasant atmosphere.

Topic 1: _____ Rationales: _____

Suggestions:

1. _____   2. _____

_____   _____

3. _____   4. _____

_____   _____

Vote   1. Yes __ / No __   2. Yes __ / No __   3. Yes __ / No __   4. Yes __ / No __

Decision: _____ Benefit: _____

Topic 2: _____ Rationales: _____

Suggestions:

1. _____   2. _____

_____   _____

3. _____   4. _____

_____   _____

Vote   1. Yes __ / No __   2. Yes __ / No __   3. Yes __ / No __   4. Yes __ / No __

Decision: _____ Benefit: _____

Family Meetings should create a tone of peace, communication, order, justice, freedom, and safety

TOPICS TO BE DISCUSSED AT THE NEXT MEETING

	Date / Name	Topic

ADDITIONAL NOTES

FAMILY MEETING
Creating Healthy Family Communication

Time Began: _____ Ended: _____ Led by: _____ Date: _____

Announcements: _____

_____

_____

Topic Examples: Family activities, family problems, standards, motivational systems, and consequences.

Rules: No pointing fingers, name calling, etc. Topics should never target a person. Those issues can be discussed in mentor meetings. When discussing rationales, decisions and benefits, keep top-of-mind: Fair, effective, love and concern, pleasant atmosphere.

Topic 1: _____ Rationales: _____

Suggestions:

1. _____   2. _____

_____   _____

3. _____   4. _____

_____   _____

Vote   1. Yes __ / No __   2. Yes __ / No __   3. Yes __ / No __   4. Yes __ / No __

Decision: _____ Benefit: _____

Topic 2: _____ Rationales: _____

Suggestions:

1. _____   2. _____

_____   _____

3. _____   4. _____

_____   _____

Vote   1. Yes __ / No __   2. Yes __ / No __   3. Yes __ / No __   4. Yes __ / No __

Decision: _____ Benefit: _____

Family Meetings should create a tone of peace, communication, order, justice, freedom, and safety

TOPICS TO BE DISCUSSED AT THE NEXT MEETING

	Date / Name	Topic

ADDITIONAL NOTES

FAMILY MEETING
Creating Healthy Family Communication

Time Began: _____ Ended: _____ Led by: _____ Date: _____

Announcements: _____

_____

_____

Topic Examples: Family activities, family problems, standards, motivational systems, and consequences.

Rules: No pointing fingers, name calling, etc. Topics should never target a person. Those issues can be discussed in mentor meetings. When discussing rationales, decisions and benefits, keep top-of-mind: Fair, effective, love and concern, pleasant atmosphere.

Topic 1: _____ Rationales: _____

Suggestions:

1. _____   2. _____

_____   _____

3. _____   4. _____

_____   _____

Vote   1. Yes __ / No __   2. Yes __ / No __   3. Yes __ / No __   4. Yes __ / No __

Decision: _____ Benefit: _____

Topic 2: _____ Rationales: _____

Suggestions:

1. _____   2. _____

_____   _____

3. _____   4. _____

_____   _____

Vote   1. Yes __ / No __   2. Yes __ / No __   3. Yes __ / No __   4. Yes __ / No __

Decision: _____ Benefit: _____

Family Meetings should create a tone of peace, communication, order, justice, freedom, and safety

TOPICS TO BE DISCUSSED AT THE NEXT MEETING

	Date / Name	Topic

ADDITIONAL NOTES

FAMILY MEETING

Creating Healthy Family Communication

Time Began: _____ Ended: _____ Led by: _____ Date: _____

Announcements: _____

_____

_____

Topic Examples: Family activities, family problems, standards, motivational systems, and consequences.

Rules: No pointing fingers, name calling, etc. Topics should never target a person. Those issues can be discussed in mentor meetings. When discussing rationales, decisions and benefits, keep top-of-mind: Fair, effective, love and concern, pleasant atmosphere.

Topic 1: _____ Rationales: _____

Suggestions:

1. _____   2. _____

_____   _____

3. _____   4. _____

_____   _____

Vote   1. Yes __ / No __   2. Yes __ / No __   3. Yes __ / No __   4. Yes __ / No __

Decision: _____ Benefit: _____

Topic 2: _____ Rationales: _____

Suggestions:

1. _____   2. _____

_____   _____

3. _____   4. _____

_____   _____

Vote   1. Yes __ / No __   2. Yes __ / No __   3. Yes __ / No __   4. Yes __ / No __

Decision: _____ Benefit: _____

Family Meetings should create a tone of peace, communication, order, justice, freedom, and safety

TOPICS TO BE DISCUSSED AT THE NEXT MEETING

	Date / Name	Topic

ADDITIONAL NOTES

FAMILY MEETING
Creating Healthy Family Communication

Time Began: _____ Ended: _____ Led by: _____ Date: _____

Announcements: _____

_____

_____

Topic Examples: Family activities, family problems, standards, motivational systems, and consequences.

Rules: No pointing fingers, name calling, etc. Topics should never target a person. Those issues can be discussed in mentor meetings. When discussing rationales, decisions and benefits, keep top-of-mind: Fair, effective, love and concern, pleasant atmosphere.

Topic 1: _____   Rationales: _____

Suggestions:

1. _____   2. _____

_____   _____

3. _____   4. _____

_____   _____

Vote   1. Yes __ / No __   2. Yes __ / No __   3. Yes __ / No __   4. Yes __ / No __

Decision: _____   Benefit: _____

Topic 2: _____   Rationales: _____

Suggestions:

1. _____   2. _____

_____   _____

3. _____   4. _____

_____   _____

Vote   1. Yes __ / No __   2. Yes __ / No __   3. Yes __ / No __   4. Yes __ / No __

Decision: _____   Benefit: _____

Family Meetings should create a tone of peace, communication, order, justice, freedom, and safety

TOPICS TO BE DISCUSSED AT THE NEXT MEETING

	Date / Name	Topic

ADDITIONAL NOTES

FAMILY MEETING

Creating Healthy Family Communication

Time Began: _____ Ended: _____ Led by: _____ Date: _____

Announcements: _____

_____

_____

Topic Examples: Family activities, family problems, standards, motivational systems, and consequences.

Rules: No pointing fingers, name calling, etc. Topics should never target a person. Those issues can be discussed in mentor meetings. When discussing rationales, decisions and benefits, keep top-of-mind: Fair, effective, love and concern, pleasant atmosphere.

Topic 1: _____ Rationales: _____

Suggestions:

1. _____ 2. _____

_____ _____

3. _____ 4. _____

_____ _____

Vote   1. Yes __ / No __   2. Yes __ / No __   3. Yes __ / No __   4. Yes __ / No __

Decision: _____ Benefit: _____

Topic 2: _____ Rationales: _____

Suggestions:

1. _____ 2. _____

_____ _____

3. _____ 4. _____

_____ _____

Vote   1. Yes __ / No __   2. Yes __ / No __   3. Yes __ / No __   4. Yes __ / No __

Decision: _____ Benefit: _____

Family Meetings should create a tone of peace, communication, order, justice, freedom, and safety

TOPICS TO BE DISCUSSED AT THE NEXT MEETING

	Date / Name	Topic

ADDITIONAL NOTES

FAMILY MEETING

Creating Healthy Family Communication

Time Began: _____ Ended: _____ Led by: _____ Date: _____

Announcements: _____

_____

_____

Topic Examples: Family activities, family problems, standards, motivational systems, and consequences.

Rules: No pointing fingers, name calling, etc. Topics should never target a person. Those issues can be discussed in mentor meetings. When discussing rationales, decisions and benefits, keep top-of-mind: Fair, effective, love and concern, pleasant atmosphere.

Topic 1: _____ Rationales: _____

Suggestions:

1. _____ 2. _____

_____ _____

3. _____ 4. _____

_____ _____

Vote   1. Yes __ / No __   2. Yes __ / No __   3. Yes __ / No __   4. Yes __ / No __

Decision: _____ Benefit: _____

Topic 2: _____ Rationales: _____

Suggestions:

1. _____ 2. _____

_____ _____

3. _____ 4. _____

_____ _____

Vote   1. Yes __ / No __   2. Yes __ / No __   3. Yes __ / No __   4. Yes __ / No __

Decision: _____ Benefit: _____

Family Meetings should create a tone of peace, communication, order, justice, freedom, and safety

TOPICS TO BE DISCUSSED AT THE NEXT MEETING

	Date / Name	Topic

ADDITIONAL NOTES

_____

_____

_____

_____

_____

_____

_____

_____

_____

FAMILY MEETING
Creating Healthy Family Communication

Time Began: _____ Ended: _____ Led by: _____ Date: _____

Announcements: _____

_____

_____

Topic Examples: Family activities, family problems, standards, motivational systems, and consequences.

Rules: No pointing fingers, name calling, etc. Topics should never target a person. Those issues can be discussed in mentor meetings. When discussing rationales, decisions and benefits, keep top-of-mind: Fair, effective, love and concern, pleasant atmosphere.

Topic 1: _____ Rationales: _____

Suggestions:

1. _____ 2. _____

_____ _____

3. _____ 4. _____

_____ _____

Vote   1. Yes __ / No __   2. Yes __ / No __   3. Yes __ / No __   4. Yes __ / No __

Decision: _____ Benefit: _____

Topic 2: _____ Rationales: _____

Suggestions:

1. _____ 2. _____

_____ _____

3. _____ 4. _____

_____ _____

Vote   1. Yes __ / No __   2. Yes __ / No __   3. Yes __ / No __   4. Yes __ / No __

Decision: _____ Benefit: _____

Family Meetings should create a tone of peace, communication, order, justice, freedom, and safety

TOPICS TO BE DISCUSSED AT THE NEXT MEETING

	Date / Name	Topic

ADDITIONAL NOTES

FAMILY MEETING

Creating Healthy Family Communication

Time Began: _____ Ended: _____ Led by: _____ Date: _____

Announcements: _____

_____

_____

Topic Examples: Family activities, family problems, standards, motivational systems, and consequences.

Rules: No pointing fingers, name calling, etc. Topics should never target a person. Those issues can be discussed in mentor meetings. When discussing rationales, decisions and benefits, keep top-of-mind: Fair, effective, love and concern, pleasant atmosphere.

Topic 1: _____ Rationales: _____

Suggestions:

1. _____   2. _____

_____   _____

3. _____   4. _____

_____   _____

Vote   1. Yes __ / No __   2. Yes __ / No __   3. Yes __ / No __   4. Yes __ / No __

Decision: _____ Benefit: _____

Topic 2: _____ Rationales: _____

Suggestions:

1. _____   2. _____

_____   _____

3. _____   4. _____

_____   _____

Vote   1. Yes __ / No __   2. Yes __ / No __   3. Yes __ / No __   4. Yes __ / No __

Decision: _____ Benefit: _____

Family Meetings should create a tone of peace, communication, order, justice, freedom, and safety

TOPICS TO BE DISCUSSED AT THE NEXT MEETING

	Date / Name	Topic

ADDITIONAL NOTES

FAMILY MEETING

Creating Healthy Family Communication

Time Began: _____ Ended: _____ Led by: _____ Date: _____

Announcements: _____

_____

_____

Topic Examples: Family activities, family problems, standards, motivational systems, and consequences.

Rules: No pointing fingers, name calling, etc. Topics should never target a person. Those issues can be discussed in mentor meetings. When discussing rationales, decisions and benefits, keep top-of-mind: Fair, effective, love and concern, pleasant atmosphere.

Topic 1: _____ Rationales: _____

Suggestions:

1. _____   2. _____

_____   _____

3. _____   4. _____

_____   _____

Vote   1. Yes __ / No __   2. Yes __ / No __   3. Yes __ / No __   4. Yes __ / No __

Decision: _____   Benefit: _____

Topic 2: _____ Rationales: _____

Suggestions:

1. _____   2. _____

_____   _____

3. _____   4. _____

_____   _____

Vote   1. Yes __ / No __   2. Yes __ / No __   3. Yes __ / No __   4. Yes __ / No __

Decision: _____   Benefit: _____

Family Meetings should create a tone of peace, communication, order, justice, freedom, and safety

TOPICS TO BE DISCUSSED AT THE NEXT MEETING

	Date / Name	Topic

ADDITIONAL NOTES

FAMILY MEETING
Creating Healthy Family Communication

Time Began: _____ Ended: _____ Led by: _____ Date: _____

Announcements: _____

_____

_____

Topic Examples: Family activities, family problems, standards, motivational systems, and consequences.

Rules: No pointing fingers, name calling, etc. Topics should never target a person. Those issues can be discussed in mentor meetings. When discussing rationales, decisions and benefits, keep top-of-mind: Fair, effective, love and concern, pleasant atmosphere.

Topic 1: _____ Rationales: _____

Suggestions:

1. _____ 2. _____

3. _____ 4. _____

Vote 1. Yes __ / No __ 2. Yes __ / No __ 3. Yes __ / No __ 4. Yes __ / No __

Decision: _____ Benefit: _____

Topic 2: _____ Rationales: _____

Suggestions:

1. _____ 2. _____

3. _____ 4. _____

Vote 1. Yes __ / No __ 2. Yes __ / No __ 3. Yes __ / No __ 4. Yes __ / No __

Decision: _____ Benefit: _____

Family Meetings should create a tone of peace, communication, order, justice, freedom, and safety

TOPICS TO BE DISCUSSED AT THE NEXT MEETING

	Date / Name	Topic

ADDITIONAL NOTES

_____

_____

_____

_____

_____

_____

_____

_____

_____

FAMILY MEETING

Creating Healthy Family Communication

Time Began: _____ Ended: _____ Led by: _____ Date: _____

Announcements: _____

_____

_____

Topic Examples: Family activities, family problems, standards, motivational systems, and consequences.

Rules: No pointing fingers, name calling, etc. Topics should never target a person. Those issues can be discussed in mentor meetings. When discussing rationales, decisions and benefits, keep top-of-mind: Fair, effective, love and concern, pleasant atmosphere.

Topic 1: _____ Rationales: _____

Suggestions:

1. _____ 2. _____

_____ _____

3. _____ 4. _____

_____ _____

Vote   1. Yes __ / No __   2. Yes __ / No __   3. Yes __ / No __   4. Yes __ / No __

Decision: _____ Benefit: _____

Topic 2: _____ Rationales: _____

Suggestions:

1. _____ 2. _____

_____ _____

3. _____ 4. _____

_____ _____

Vote   1. Yes __ / No __   2. Yes __ / No __   3. Yes __ / No __   4. Yes __ / No __

Decision: _____ Benefit: _____

Family Meetings should create a tone of peace, communication, order, justice, freedom, and safety

TOPICS TO BE DISCUSSED AT THE NEXT MEETING

	Date / Name	Topic

ADDITIONAL NOTES

FAMILY MEETING
Creating Healthy Family Communication

Time Began: _____ Ended: _____ Led by: _____ Date: _____

Announcements: _____

_____

_____

Topic Examples: Family activities, family problems, standards, motivational systems, and consequences.

Rules: No pointing fingers, name calling, etc. Topics should never target a person. Those issues can be discussed in mentor meetings. When discussing rationales, decisions and benefits, keep top-of-mind: Fair, effective, love and concern, pleasant atmosphere.

Topic 1: _____ Rationales: _____

Suggestions:

1. _____ 2. _____

_____ _____

3. _____ 4. _____

_____ _____

Vote   1. Yes __ / No __   2. Yes __ / No __   3. Yes __ / No __   4. Yes __ / No __

Decision: _____ Benefit: _____

Topic 2: _____ Rationales: _____

Suggestions:

1. _____ 2. _____

_____ _____

3. _____ 4. _____

_____ _____

Vote   1. Yes __ / No __   2. Yes __ / No __   3. Yes __ / No __   4. Yes __ / No __

Decision: _____ Benefit: _____

Family Meetings should create a tone of peace, communication, order, justice, freedom, and safety

TOPICS TO BE DISCUSSED AT THE NEXT MEETING

	Date / Name	Topic

ADDITIONAL NOTES

FAMILY MEETING

Creating Healthy Family Communication

Time Began: _____ Ended: _____ Led by: _____ Date: _____

Announcements: _____

_____

_____

Topic Examples: Family activities, family problems, standards, motivational systems, and consequences.

Rules: No pointing fingers, name calling, etc. Topics should never target a person. Those issues can be discussed in mentor meetings. When discussing rationales, decisions and benefits, keep top-of-mind: Fair, effective, love and concern, pleasant atmosphere.

Topic 1: _____ Rationales: _____

Suggestions:

1. _____   2. _____

_____   _____

3. _____   4. _____

_____   _____

Vote   1. Yes __ / No __   2. Yes __ / No __   3. Yes __ / No __   4. Yes __ / No __

Decision: _____ Benefit: _____

Topic 2: _____ Rationales: _____

Suggestions:

1. _____   2. _____

_____   _____

3. _____   4. _____

_____   _____

Vote   1. Yes __ / No __   2. Yes __ / No __   3. Yes __ / No __   4. Yes __ / No __

Decision: _____ Benefit: _____

Family Meetings should create a tone of peace, communication, order, justice, freedom, and safety

TOPICS TO BE DISCUSSED AT THE NEXT MEETING

	Date / Name	Topic

ADDITIONAL NOTES

FAMILY MEETING
Creating Healthy Family Communication

Time Began: _____ Ended: _____ Led by: _____ Date: _____

Announcements: _____

_____

_____

Topic Examples: Family activities, family problems, standards, motivational systems, and consequences.

Rules: No pointing fingers, name calling, etc. Topics should never target a person. Those issues can be discussed in mentor meetings. When discussing rationales, decisions and benefits, keep top-of-mind: Fair, effective, love and concern, pleasant atmosphere.

Topic 1: _____ Rationales: _____

Suggestions:

1. _____   2. _____

_____   _____

3. _____   4. _____

_____   _____

Vote   1. Yes __ / No __   2. Yes __ / No __   3. Yes __ / No __   4. Yes __ / No __

Decision: _____ Benefit: _____

Topic 2: _____ Rationales: _____

Suggestions:

1. _____   2. _____

_____   _____

3. _____   4. _____

_____   _____

Vote   1. Yes __ / No __   2. Yes __ / No __   3. Yes __ / No __   4. Yes __ / No __

Decision: _____ Benefit: _____

Family Meetings should create a tone of peace, communication, order, justice, freedom, and safety

TOPICS TO BE DISCUSSED AT THE NEXT MEETING

	Date / Name	Topic

ADDITIONAL NOTES

FAMILY MEETING
Creating Healthy Family Communication

Time Began: _____ Ended: _____ Led by: _____ Date: _____

Announcements: _____

_____

_____

Topic Examples: Family activities, family problems, standards, motivational systems, and consequences.

Rules: No pointing fingers, name calling, etc. Topics should never target a person. Those issues can be discussed in mentor meetings. When discussing rationales, decisions and benefits, keep top-of-mind: Fair, effective, love and concern, pleasant atmosphere.

Topic 1: _____ Rationales: _____

Suggestions:
1. _____ 2. _____

3. _____ 4. _____

Vote   1. Yes __ / No __   2. Yes __ / No __   3. Yes __ / No __   4. Yes __ / No __

Decision: _____ Benefit: _____

Topic 2: _____ Rationales: _____

Suggestions:
1. _____ 2. _____

3. _____ 4. _____

Vote   1. Yes __ / No __   2. Yes __ / No __   3. Yes __ / No __   4. Yes __ / No __

Decision: _____ Benefit: _____

Family Meetings should create a tone of peace, communication, order, justice, freedom, and safety

TOPICS TO BE DISCUSSED AT THE NEXT MEETING

	Date / Name	Topic

ADDITIONAL NOTES

FAMILY MEETING
Creating Healthy Family Communication

Time Began: _____ Ended: _____ Led by: _____ Date: _____

Announcements: _____

_____

_____

Topic Examples: Family activities, family problems, standards, motivational systems, and consequences.

Rules: No pointing fingers, name calling, etc. Topics should never target a person. Those issues can be discussed in mentor meetings. When discussing rationales, decisions and benefits, keep top-of-mind: Fair, effective, love and concern, pleasant atmosphere.

Topic 1: _____ Rationales: _____

Suggestions:
1. _____   2. _____

   _____   _____

3. _____   4. _____

   _____   _____

Vote   1. Yes __ / No __   2. Yes __ / No __   3. Yes __ / No __   4. Yes __ / No __

Decision: _____ Benefit: _____

Topic 2: _____ Rationales: _____

Suggestions:
1. _____   2. _____

   _____   _____

3. _____   4. _____

   _____   _____

Vote   1. Yes __ / No __   2. Yes __ / No __   3. Yes __ / No __   4. Yes __ / No __

Decision: _____ Benefit: _____

Family Meetings should create a tone of peace, communication, order, justice, freedom, and safety

TOPICS TO BE DISCUSSED AT THE NEXT MEETING

	Date / Name	Topic

ADDITIONAL NOTES

FAMILY MEETING

Creating Healthy Family Communication

Time Began: _____ Ended: _____ Led by: _____ Date: _____

Announcements: _____

_____

_____

Topic Examples: Family activities, family problems, standards, motivational systems, and consequences.

Rules: No pointing fingers, name calling, etc. Topics should never target a person. Those issues can be discussed in mentor meetings. When discussing rationales, decisions and benefits, keep top-of-mind: Fair, effective, love and concern, pleasant atmosphere.

Topic 1: _____ Rationales: _____

Suggestions:

1. _____ 2. _____

   _____   _____

3. _____ 4. _____

   _____   _____

Vote   1. Yes __ / No __   2. Yes __ / No __   3. Yes __ / No __   4. Yes __ / No __

Decision: _____ Benefit: _____

Topic 2: _____ Rationales: _____

Suggestions:

1. _____ 2. _____

   _____   _____

3. _____ 4. _____

   _____   _____

Vote   1. Yes __ / No __   2. Yes __ / No __   3. Yes __ / No __   4. Yes __ / No __

Decision: _____ Benefit: _____

Family Meetings should create a tone of peace, communication, order, justice, freedom, and safety

TOPICS TO BE DISCUSSED AT THE NEXT MEETING

	Date / Name	Topic

ADDITIONAL NOTES

FAMILY MEETING
Creating Healthy Family Communication

Time Began: _____ Ended: _____ Led by: _____ Date: _____

Announcements: _____

_____

_____

Topic Examples: Family activities, family problems, standards, motivational systems, and consequences.

Rules: No pointing fingers, name calling, etc. Topics should never target a person. Those issues can be discussed in mentor meetings. When discussing rationales, decisions and benefits, keep top-of-mind: Fair, effective, love and concern, pleasant atmosphere.

Topic 1: _____ Rationales: _____

Suggestions:

1. _____ 2. _____

_____ _____

3. _____ 4. _____

_____ _____

Vote   1. Yes __ / No __   2. Yes __ / No __   3. Yes __ / No __   4. Yes __ / No __

Decision: _____ Benefit: _____

Topic 2: _____ Rationales: _____

Suggestions:

1. _____ 2. _____

_____ _____

3. _____ 4. _____

_____ _____

Vote   1. Yes __ / No __   2. Yes __ / No __   3. Yes __ / No __   4. Yes __ / No __

Decision: _____ Benefit: _____

Family Meetings should create a tone of peace, communication, order, justice, freedom, and safety

TOPICS TO BE DISCUSSED AT THE NEXT MEETING

	Date / Name	Topic

ADDITIONAL NOTES

FAMILY MEETING
Creating Healthy Family Communication

Time Began: _____ Ended: _____ Led by: _____ Date: _____

Announcements: _____

_____

_____

Topic Examples: Family activities, family problems, standards, motivational systems, and consequences.

Rules: No pointing fingers, name calling, etc. Topics should never target a person. Those issues can be discussed in mentor meetings. When discussing rationales, decisions and benefits, keep top-of-mind: Fair, effective, love and concern, pleasant atmosphere.

Topic 1: _____ Rationales: _____

Suggestions:

1. _____ 2. _____

_____ _____

3. _____ 4. _____

_____ _____

Vote   1. Yes __ / No __   2. Yes __ / No __   3. Yes __ / No __   4. Yes __ / No __

Decision: _____ Benefit: _____

Topic 2: _____ Rationales: _____

Suggestions:

1. _____ 2. _____

_____ _____

3. _____ 4. _____

_____ _____

Vote   1. Yes __ / No __   2. Yes __ / No __   3. Yes __ / No __   4. Yes __ / No __

Decision: _____ Benefit: _____

Family Meetings should create a tone of peace, communication, order, justice, freedom, and safety

TOPICS TO BE DISCUSSED AT THE NEXT MEETING

	Date / Name	Topic

ADDITIONAL NOTES

FAMILY MEETING

Creating Healthy Family Communication

Time Began: _____ Ended: _____ Led by: _____ Date: _____

Announcements: _____

_____

_____

Topic Examples: Family activities, family problems, standards, motivational systems, and consequences.

Rules: No pointing fingers, name calling, etc. Topics should never target a person. Those issues can be discussed in mentor meetings. When discussing rationales, decisions and benefits, keep top-of-mind: Fair, effective, love and concern, pleasant atmosphere.

Topic 1: _____ Rationales: _____

Suggestions:

1. _____   2. _____

   _____   _____

3. _____   4. _____

   _____   _____

Vote   1. Yes __ / No __   2. Yes __ / No __   3. Yes __ / No __   4. Yes __ / No __

Decision: _____ Benefit: _____

Topic 2: _____ Rationales: _____

Suggestions:

1. _____   2. _____

   _____   _____

3. _____   4. _____

   _____   _____

Vote   1. Yes __ / No __   2. Yes __ / No __   3. Yes __ / No __   4. Yes __ / No __

Decision: _____ Benefit: _____

Family Meetings should create a tone of peace, communication, order, justice, freedom, and safety

TOPICS TO BE DISCUSSED AT THE NEXT MEETING

	Date / Name	Topic

ADDITIONAL NOTES

_____

_____

_____

_____

_____

_____

_____

_____

_____

_____

FAMILY MEETING
Creating Healthy Family Communication

Time Began: _____ Ended: _____ Led by: _____ Date: _____

Announcements: _____

_____

_____

Topic Examples: Family activities, family problems, standards, motivational systems, and consequences.

Rules: No pointing fingers, name calling, etc. Topics should never target a person. Those issues can be discussed in mentor meetings. When discussing rationales, decisions and benefits, keep top-of-mind: Fair, effective, love and concern, pleasant atmosphere.

Topic 1: _____ Rationales: _____

Suggestions:

1. _____   2. _____

    _____   _____

3. _____   4. _____

    _____   _____

Vote   1. Yes __ / No __   2. Yes __ / No __   3. Yes __ / No __   4. Yes __ / No __

Decision: _____ Benefit: _____

Topic 2: _____ Rationales: _____

Suggestions:

1. _____   2. _____

    _____   _____

3. _____   4. _____

    _____   _____

Vote   1. Yes __ / No __   2. Yes __ / No __   3. Yes __ / No __   4. Yes __ / No __

Decision: _____ Benefit: _____

Family Meetings should create a tone of peace, communication, order, justice, freedom, and safety

TOPICS TO BE DISCUSSED AT THE NEXT MEETING

	Date / Name	Topic

ADDITIONAL NOTES

_____

_____

_____

_____

_____

_____

_____

_____

_____

_____

FAMILY MEETING
Creating Healthy Family Communication

Time Began: _____ Ended: _____ Led by: _____ Date: _____

Announcements: _____

_____

_____

Topic Examples: Family activities, family problems, standards, motivational systems, and consequences.

Rules: No pointing fingers, name calling, etc. Topics should never target a person. Those issues can be discussed in mentor meetings. When discussing rationales, decisions and benefits, keep top-of-mind: Fair, effective, love and concern, pleasant atmosphere.

Topic 1: _____ Rationales: _____

Suggestions:

1. _____   2. _____

_____   _____

3. _____   4. _____

_____   _____

Vote   1. Yes __ / No __   2. Yes __ / No __   3. Yes __ / No __   4. Yes __ / No __

Decision: _____ Benefit: _____

Topic 2: _____ Rationales: _____

Suggestions:

1. _____   2. _____

_____   _____

3. _____   4. _____

_____   _____

Vote   1. Yes __ / No __   2. Yes __ / No __   3. Yes __ / No __   4. Yes __ / No __

Decision: _____ Benefit: _____

Family Meetings should create a tone of peace, communication, order, justice, freedom, and safety

TOPICS TO BE DISCUSSED AT THE NEXT MEETING

	Date / Name	Topic

ADDITIONAL NOTES

FAMILY MEETING
Creating Healthy Family Communication

Time Began: _____ Ended: _____ Led by: _____ Date: _____

Announcements: _____

_____

_____

Topic Examples: Family activities, family problems, standards, motivational systems, and consequences.

Rules: No pointing fingers, name calling, etc. Topics should never target a person. Those issues can be discussed in mentor meetings. When discussing rationales, decisions and benefits, keep top-of-mind: Fair, effective, love and concern, pleasant atmosphere.

Topic 1: _____ Rationales: _____

Suggestions:

1. _____ 2. _____

_____ _____

3. _____ 4. _____

_____ _____

Vote   1. Yes __ / No __   2. Yes __ / No __   3. Yes __ / No __   4. Yes __ / No __

Decision: _____ Benefit: _____

Topic 2: _____ Rationales: _____

Suggestions:

1. _____ 2. _____

_____ _____

3. _____ 4. _____

_____ _____

Vote   1. Yes __ / No __   2. Yes __ / No __   3. Yes __ / No __   4. Yes __ / No __

Decision: _____ Benefit: _____

Family Meetings should create a tone of peace, communication, order, justice, freedom, and safety

TOPICS TO BE DISCUSSED AT THE NEXT MEETING

	Date / Name	Topic

ADDITIONAL NOTES

FAMILY MEETING
Creating Healthy Family Communication

Time Began: _____ Ended: _____ Led by: _____ Date: _____

Announcements: _____

_____

_____

Topic Examples: Family activities, family problems, standards, motivational systems, and consequences.

Rules: No pointing fingers, name calling, etc. Topics should never target a person. Those issues can be discussed in mentor meetings. When discussing rationales, decisions and benefits, keep top-of-mind: Fair, effective, love and concern, pleasant atmosphere.

Topic 1: _____ Rationales: _____

Suggestions:
1. _____ 2. _____

_____ _____

3. _____ 4. _____

_____ _____

Vote   1. Yes __ / No __   2. Yes __ / No __   3. Yes __ / No __   4. Yes __ / No __

Decision: _____ Benefit: _____

Topic 2: _____ Rationales: _____

Suggestions:
1. _____ 2. _____

_____ _____

3. _____ 4. _____

_____ _____

Vote   1. Yes __ / No __   2. Yes __ / No __   3. Yes __ / No __   4. Yes __ / No __

Decision: _____ Benefit: _____

Family Meetings should create a tone of peace, communication, order, justice, freedom, and safety

TOPICS TO BE DISCUSSED AT THE NEXT MEETING

	Date / Name	Topic

ADDITIONAL NOTES

_____

_____

_____

_____

_____

_____

_____

_____

_____

_____

FAMILY MEETING
Creating Healthy Family Communication

Time Began: _____ Ended: _____ Led by: _____ Date: _____

Announcements: _____

_____

_____

Topic Examples: Family activities, family problems, standards, motivational systems, and consequences.

Rules: No pointing fingers, name calling, etc. Topics should never target a person. Those issues can be discussed in mentor meetings. When discussing rationales, decisions and benefits, keep top-of-mind: Fair, effective, love and concern, pleasant atmosphere.

Topic 1: _____ Rationales: _____

Suggestions:

1. _____   2. _____

_____   _____

3. _____   4. _____

_____   _____

Vote   1. Yes __ / No __   2. Yes __ / No __   3. Yes __ / No __   4. Yes __ / No __

Decision: _____ Benefit: _____

Topic 2: _____ Rationales: _____

Suggestions:

1. _____   2. _____

_____   _____

3. _____   4. _____

_____   _____

Vote   1. Yes __ / No __   2. Yes __ / No __   3. Yes __ / No __   4. Yes __ / No __

Decision: _____ Benefit: _____

Family Meetings should create a tone of peace, communication, order, justice, freedom, and safety

TOPICS TO BE DISCUSSED AT THE NEXT MEETING

	Date / Name	Topic

ADDITIONAL NOTES

_____

_____

_____

_____

_____

_____

_____

_____

_____

_____

FAMILY MEETING
Creating Healthy Family Communication

Time Began: _____ Ended: _____ Led by: _____ Date: _____

Announcements: _____

_____

_____

Topic Examples: Family activities, family problems, standards, motivational systems, and consequences.

Rules: No pointing fingers, name calling, etc. Topics should never target a person. Those issues can be discussed in mentor meetings. When discussing rationales, decisions and benefits, keep top-of-mind: Fair, effective, love and concern, pleasant atmosphere.

Topic 1: _____ Rationales: _____

Suggestions:

1. _____ 2. _____

_____ _____

3. _____ 4. _____

_____ _____

Vote   1. Yes __ / No __   2. Yes __ / No __   3. Yes __ / No __   4. Yes __ / No __

Decision: _____ Benefit: _____

Topic 2: _____ Rationales: _____

Suggestions:

1. _____ 2. _____

_____ _____

3. _____ 4. _____

_____ _____

Vote   1. Yes __ / No __   2. Yes __ / No __   3. Yes __ / No __   4. Yes __ / No __

Decision: _____ Benefit: _____

Family Meetings should create a tone of peace, communication, order, justice, freedom, and safety

TOPICS TO BE DISCUSSED AT THE NEXT MEETING

	Date / Name	Topic

ADDITIONAL NOTES

FAMILY MEETING

Creating Healthy Family Communication

Time Began: _____ Ended: _____ Led by: _____ Date: _____

Announcements: _____

_____

_____

Topic Examples: Family activities, family problems, standards, motivational systems, and consequences.

Rules: No pointing fingers, name calling, etc. Topics should never target a person. Those issues can be discussed in mentor meetings. When discussing rationales, decisions and benefits, keep top-of-mind: Fair, effective, love and concern, pleasant atmosphere.

Topic 1: _____ Rationales: _____

Suggestions:

1. _____ 2. _____

_____ _____

3. _____ 4. _____

_____ _____

Vote   1. Yes __ / No __   2. Yes __ / No __   3. Yes __ / No __   4. Yes __ / No __

Decision: _____ Benefit: _____

Topic 2: _____ Rationales: _____

Suggestions:

1. _____ 2. _____

_____ _____

3. _____ 4. _____

_____ _____

Vote   1. Yes __ / No __   2. Yes __ / No __   3. Yes __ / No __   4. Yes __ / No __

Decision: _____ Benefit: _____

Family Meetings should create a tone of peace, communication, order, justice, freedom, and safety

TOPICS TO BE DISCUSSED AT THE NEXT MEETING

	Date / Name	Topic

ADDITIONAL NOTES

FAMILY MEETING

Creating Healthy Family Communication

Time Began: _____ Ended: _____ Led by: _____ Date: _____

Announcements: _____

_____

_____

Topic Examples: Family activities, family problems, standards, motivational systems, and consequences.

Rules: No pointing fingers, name calling, etc. Topics should never target a person. Those issues can be discussed in mentor meetings. When discussing rationales, decisions and benefits, keep top-of-mind: Fair, effective, love and concern, pleasant atmosphere.

Topic 1: _____ Rationales: _____

Suggestions:

1. _____   2. _____

_____   _____

3. _____   4. _____

_____   _____

Vote   1. Yes __ / No __   2. Yes __ / No __   3. Yes __ / No __   4. Yes __ / No __

Decision: _____ Benefit: _____

Topic 2: _____ Rationales: _____

Suggestions:

1. _____   2. _____

_____   _____

3. _____   4. _____

_____   _____

Vote   1. Yes __ / No __   2. Yes __ / No __   3. Yes __ / No __   4. Yes __ / No __

Decision: _____ Benefit: _____

Family Meetings should create a tone of peace, communication, order, justice, freedom, and safety

TOPICS TO BE DISCUSSED AT THE NEXT MEETING

	Date / Name	Topic

ADDITIONAL NOTES

FAMILY MEETING
Creating Healthy Family Communication

Time Began: _____ Ended: _____ Led by: _____ Date: _____

Announcements: _____

_____

_____

Topic Examples: Family activities, family problems, standards, motivational systems, and consequences.

Rules: No pointing fingers, name calling, etc. Topics should never target a person. Those issues can be discussed in mentor meetings. When discussing rationales, decisions and benefits, keep top-of-mind: Fair, effective, love and concern, pleasant atmosphere.

Topic 1: _____ Rationales: _____

Suggestions:

1. _____ 2. _____

_____ _____

3. _____ 4. _____

_____ _____

Vote   1. Yes __ / No __   2. Yes __ / No __   3. Yes __ / No __   4. Yes __ / No __

Decision: _____ Benefit: _____

Topic 2: _____ Rationales: _____

Suggestions:

1. _____ 2. _____

_____ _____

3. _____ 4. _____

_____ _____

Vote   1. Yes __ / No __   2. Yes __ / No __   3. Yes __ / No __   4. Yes __ / No __

Decision: _____ Benefit: _____

Family Meetings should create a tone of peace, communication, order, justice, freedom, and safety

TOPICS TO BE DISCUSSED AT THE NEXT MEETING

	Date / Name	Topic

ADDITIONAL NOTES

FAMILY MEETING
Creating Healthy Family Communication

Time Began: _____ Ended: _____ Led by: _____ Date: _____

Announcements: _____

_____

_____

Topic Examples: Family activities, family problems, standards, motivational systems, and consequences.

Rules: No pointing fingers, name calling, etc. Topics should never target a person. Those issues can be discussed in mentor meetings. When discussing rationales, decisions and benefits, keep top-of-mind: Fair, effective, love and concern, pleasant atmosphere.

Topic 1: _____ Rationales: _____

Suggestions:

1. _____   2. _____

_____   _____

3. _____   4. _____

_____   _____

Vote   1. Yes __ / No __   2. Yes __ / No __   3. Yes __ / No __   4. Yes __ / No __

Decision: _____ Benefit: _____

Topic 2: _____ Rationales: _____

Suggestions:

1. _____   2. _____

_____   _____

3. _____   4. _____

_____   _____

Vote   1. Yes __ / No __   2. Yes __ / No __   3. Yes __ / No __   4. Yes __ / No __

Decision: _____ Benefit: _____

Family Meetings should create a tone of peace, communication, order, justice, freedom, and safety

TOPICS TO BE DISCUSSED AT THE NEXT MEETING

	Date / Name	Topic

ADDITIONAL NOTES

FAMILY MEETING
Creating Healthy Family Communication

Time Began: _____ Ended: _____ Led by: _____ Date: _____

Announcements: _____

_____

_____

Topic Examples: Family activities, family problems, standards, motivational systems, and consequences.

Rules: No pointing fingers, name calling, etc. Topics should never target a person. Those issues can be discussed in mentor meetings. When discussing rationales, decisions and benefits, keep top-of-mind: Fair, effective, love and concern, pleasant atmosphere.

Topic 1: _____ Rationales: _____

Suggestions:

1. _____   2. _____

_____   _____

3. _____   4. _____

_____   _____

Vote   1. Yes ___ / No ___   2. Yes ___ / No ___   3. Yes ___ / No ___   4. Yes ___ / No ___

Decision: _____ Benefit: _____

Topic 2: _____ Rationales: _____

Suggestions:

1. _____   2. _____

_____   _____

3. _____   4. _____

_____   _____

Vote   1. Yes ___ / No ___   2. Yes ___ / No ___   3. Yes ___ / No ___   4. Yes ___ / No ___

Decision: _____ Benefit: _____

Family Meetings should create a tone of peace, communication, order, justice, freedom, and safety

TOPICS TO BE DISCUSSED AT THE NEXT MEETING

	Date / Name	Topic

ADDITIONAL NOTES

FAMILY MEETING

Creating Healthy Family Communication

Time Began: _____ Ended: _____ Led by: _____ Date: _____

Announcements: _____

_____

_____

Topic Examples: Family activities, family problems, standards, motivational systems, and consequences.

Rules: No pointing fingers, name calling, etc. Topics should never target a person. Those issues can be discussed in mentor meetings. When discussing rationales, decisions and benefits, keep top-of-mind: Fair, effective, love and concern, pleasant atmosphere.

Topic 1: _____ Rationales: _____

Suggestions:

1. _____   2. _____

_____   _____

3. _____   4. _____

_____   _____

Vote   1. Yes __ / No __   2. Yes __ / No __   3. Yes __ / No __   4. Yes __ / No __

Decision: _____ Benefit: _____

Topic 2: _____ Rationales: _____

Suggestions:

1. _____   2. _____

_____   _____

3. _____   4. _____

_____   _____

Vote   1. Yes __ / No __   2. Yes __ / No __   3. Yes __ / No __   4. Yes __ / No __

Decision: _____ Benefit: _____

Family Meetings should create a tone of peace, communication, order, justice, freedom, and safety

TOPICS TO BE DISCUSSED AT THE NEXT MEETING

	Date / Name	Topic

ADDITIONAL NOTES

FAMILY MEETING
Creating Healthy Family Communication

Time Began: _____ Ended: _____ Led by: _____ Date: _____

Announcements: _____

_____

_____

Topic Examples: Family activities, family problems, standards, motivational systems, and consequences.

Rules: No pointing fingers, name calling, etc. Topics should never target a person. Those issues can be discussed in mentor meetings. When discussing rationales, decisions and benefits, keep top-of-mind: Fair, effective, love and concern, pleasant atmosphere.

Topic 1: _____   Rationales: _____

Suggestions:

1. _____   2. _____

_____   _____

3. _____   4. _____

_____   _____

Vote   1. Yes __ / No __   2. Yes __ / No __   3. Yes __ / No __   4. Yes __ / No __

Decision: _____   Benefit: _____

Topic 2: _____   Rationales: _____

Suggestions:

1. _____   2. _____

_____   _____

3. _____   4. _____

_____   _____

Vote   1. Yes __ / No __   2. Yes __ / No __   3. Yes __ / No __   4. Yes __ / No __

Decision: _____   Benefit: _____

Family Meetings should create a tone of peace, communication, order, justice, freedom, and safety

TOPICS TO BE DISCUSSED AT THE NEXT MEETING

	Date / Name	Topic

ADDITIONAL NOTES

FAMILY MEETING

Creating Healthy Family Communication

Time Began: _____ Ended: _____ Led by: _____ Date: _____

Announcements: _____

_____

_____

Topic Examples: Family activities, family problems, standards, motivational systems, and consequences.

Rules: No pointing fingers, name calling, etc. Topics should never target a person. Those issues can be discussed in mentor meetings. When discussing rationales, decisions and benefits, keep top-of-mind: Fair, effective, love and concern, pleasant atmosphere.

Topic 1: _____ Rationales: _____

Suggestions:

1. _____   2. _____

   _____   _____

3. _____   4. _____

   _____   _____

Vote   1. Yes __ / No __   2. Yes __ / No __   3. Yes __ / No __   4. Yes __ / No __

Decision: _____ Benefit: _____

Topic 2: _____ Rationales: _____

Suggestions:

1. _____   2. _____

   _____   _____

3. _____   4. _____

   _____   _____

Vote   1. Yes __ / No __   2. Yes __ / No __   3. Yes __ / No __   4. Yes __ / No __

Decision: _____ Benefit: _____

Family Meetings should create a tone of peace, communication, order, justice, freedom, and safety

TOPICS TO BE DISCUSSED AT THE NEXT MEETING

	Date / Name	Topic

ADDITIONAL NOTES

FAMILY MEETING

Creating Healthy Family Communication

Time Began: _____ Ended: _____ Led by: _____ Date: _____

Announcements: _____

_____

_____

Topic Examples: Family activities, family problems, standards, motivational systems, and consequences.

Rules: No pointing fingers, name calling, etc. Topics should never target a person. Those issues can be discussed in mentor meetings. When discussing rationales, decisions and benefits, keep top-of-mind: Fair, effective, love and concern, pleasant atmosphere.

Topic 1: _____ Rationales: _____

Suggestions:

1. _____   2. _____

3. _____   4. _____

Vote   1. Yes __ / No __   2. Yes __ / No __   3. Yes __ / No __   4. Yes __ / No __

Decision: _____ Benefit: _____

Topic 2: _____ Rationales: _____

Suggestions:

1. _____   2. _____

3. _____   4. _____

Vote   1. Yes __ / No __   2. Yes __ / No __   3. Yes __ / No __   4. Yes __ / No __

Decision: _____ Benefit: _____

Family Meetings should create a tone of peace, communication, order, justice, freedom, and safety

TOPICS TO BE DISCUSSED AT THE NEXT MEETING

	Date / Name	Topic

ADDITIONAL NOTES

FAMILY MEETING
Creating Healthy Family Communication

Time Began: _____ Ended: _____ Led by: _____ Date: _____

Announcements: _____

_____

_____

Topic Examples: Family activities, family problems, standards, motivational systems, and consequences.

Rules: No pointing fingers, name calling, etc. Topics should never target a person. Those issues can be discussed in mentor meetings. When discussing rationales, decisions and benefits, keep top-of-mind: Fair, effective, love and concern, pleasant atmosphere.

Topic 1: _____ Rationales: _____

Suggestions:

1. _____   2. _____

_____   _____

3. _____   4. _____

_____   _____

Vote   1. Yes __ / No __   2. Yes __ / No __   3. Yes __ / No __   4. Yes __ / No __

Decision: _____ Benefit: _____

Topic 2: _____ Rationales: _____

Suggestions:

1. _____   2. _____

_____   _____

3. _____   4. _____

_____   _____

Vote   1. Yes __ / No __   2. Yes __ / No __   3. Yes __ / No __   4. Yes __ / No __

Decision: _____ Benefit: _____

Family Meetings should create a tone of peace, communication, order, justice, freedom, and safety

TOPICS TO BE DISCUSSED AT THE NEXT MEETING

	Date / Name	Topic

ADDITIONAL NOTES

FAMILY MEETING
Creating Healthy Family Communication

Time Began: _____ Ended: _____ Led by: _____ Date: _____

Announcements: _____

_____

_____

Topic Examples: Family activities, family problems, standards, motivational systems, and consequences.

Rules: No pointing fingers, name calling, etc. Topics should never target a person. Those issues can be discussed in mentor meetings. When discussing rationales, decisions and benefits, keep top-of-mind: Fair, effective, love and concern, pleasant atmosphere.

Topic 1: _____ Rationales: _____

Suggestions:

1. _____   2. _____

_____   _____

3. _____   4. _____

_____   _____

Vote   1. Yes __ / No __   2. Yes __ / No __   3. Yes __ / No __   4. Yes __ / No __

Decision: _____ Benefit: _____

Topic 2: _____ Rationales: _____

Suggestions:

1. _____   2. _____

_____   _____

3. _____   4. _____

_____   _____

Vote   1. Yes __ / No __   2. Yes __ / No __   3. Yes __ / No __   4. Yes __ / No __

Decision: _____ Benefit: _____

Family Meetings should create a tone of peace, communication, order, justice, freedom, and safety

TOPICS TO BE DISCUSSED AT THE NEXT MEETING

	Date / Name	Topic

ADDITIONAL NOTES

_____

_____

_____

_____

_____

_____

_____

_____

_____

_____

FAMILY MEETING
Creating Healthy Family Communication

Time Began: _____ Ended: _____ Led by: _____ Date: _____

Announcements: _____

_____

_____

Topic Examples: Family activities, family problems, standards, motivational systems, and consequences.

Rules: No pointing fingers, name calling, etc. Topics should never target a person. Those issues can be discussed in mentor meetings. When discussing rationales, decisions and benefits, keep top-of-mind: Fair, effective, love and concern, pleasant atmosphere.

Topic 1: _____ Rationales: _____

Suggestions:

1. _____ 2. _____

_____ _____

3. _____ 4. _____

_____ _____

Vote   1. Yes __ / No __   2. Yes __ / No __   3. Yes __ / No __   4. Yes __ / No __

Decision: _____ Benefit: _____

Topic 2: _____ Rationales: _____

Suggestions:

1. _____ 2. _____

_____ _____

3. _____ 4. _____

_____ _____

Vote   1. Yes __ / No __   2. Yes __ / No __   3. Yes __ / No __   4. Yes __ / No __

Decision: _____ Benefit: _____

Family Meetings should create a tone of peace, communication, order, justice, freedom, and safety

TOPICS TO BE DISCUSSED AT THE NEXT MEETING

	Date / Name	Topic

ADDITIONAL NOTES

FAMILY MEETING
Creating Healthy Family Communication

Time Began: _____ Ended: _____ Led by: _____ Date: _____

Announcements: _____

_____

_____

Topic Examples: Family activities, family problems, standards, motivational systems, and consequences.

Rules: No pointing fingers, name calling, etc. Topics should never target a person. Those issues can be discussed in mentor meetings. When discussing rationales, decisions and benefits, keep top-of-mind: Fair, effective, love and concern, pleasant atmosphere.

Topic 1: _____ Rationales: _____

Suggestions:

1. _____   2. _____

   _____   _____

3. _____   4. _____

   _____   _____

Vote   1. Yes __ / No __   2. Yes __ / No __   3. Yes __ / No __   4. Yes __ / No __

Decision: _____ Benefit: _____

Topic 2: _____ Rationales: _____

Suggestions:

1. _____   2. _____

   _____   _____

3. _____   4. _____

   _____   _____

Vote   1. Yes __ / No __   2. Yes __ / No __   3. Yes __ / No __   4. Yes __ / No __

Decision: _____ Benefit: _____

Family Meetings should create a tone of peace, communication, order, justice, freedom, and safety

TOPICS TO BE DISCUSSED AT THE NEXT MEETING

	Date / Name	Topic

ADDITIONAL NOTES

FAMILY MEETING

Creating Healthy Family Communication

Time Began: _____ Ended: _____ Led by: _____ Date: _____

Announcements: _____

_____

_____

Topic Examples: Family activities, family problems, standards, motivational systems, and consequences.

Rules: No pointing fingers, name calling, etc. Topics should never target a person. Those issues can be discussed in mentor meetings. When discussing rationales, decisions and benefits, keep top-of-mind: Fair, effective, love and concern, pleasant atmosphere.

Topic 1: _____ Rationales: _____

Suggestions:

1. _____ 2. _____

_____ _____

3. _____ 4. _____

_____ _____

Vote   1. Yes __ / No __   2. Yes __ / No __   3. Yes __ / No __   4. Yes __ / No __

Decision: _____ Benefit: _____

Topic 2: _____ Rationales: _____

Suggestions:

1. _____ 2. _____

_____ _____

3. _____ 4. _____

_____ _____

Vote   1. Yes __ / No __   2. Yes __ / No __   3. Yes __ / No __   4. Yes __ / No __

Decision: _____ Benefit: _____

Family Meetings should create a tone of peace, communication, order, justice, freedom, and safety

TOPICS TO BE DISCUSSED AT THE NEXT MEETING

	Date / Name	Topic

ADDITIONAL NOTES

FAMILY MEETING
Creating Healthy Family Communication

Time Began: _____ Ended: _____ Led by: _____ Date: _____

Announcements: _____

_____

_____

Topic Examples: Family activities, family problems, standards, motivational systems, and consequences.

Rules: No pointing fingers, name calling, etc. Topics should never target a person. Those issues can be discussed in mentor meetings. When discussing rationales, decisions and benefits, keep top-of-mind: Fair, effective, love and concern, pleasant atmosphere.

Topic 1: _____ Rationales: _____

Suggestions:
1. _____ 2. _____

_____ _____

3. _____ 4. _____

_____ _____

Vote   1. Yes __ / No __   2. Yes __ / No __   3. Yes __ / No __   4. Yes __ / No __

Decision: _____ Benefit: _____

Topic 2: _____ Rationales: _____

Suggestions:
1. _____ 2. _____

_____ _____

3. _____ 4. _____

_____ _____

Vote   1. Yes __ / No __   2. Yes __ / No __   3. Yes __ / No __   4. Yes __ / No __

Decision: _____ Benefit: _____

Family Meetings should create a tone of peace, communication, order, justice, freedom, and safety

TOPICS TO BE DISCUSSED AT THE NEXT MEETING

	Date / Name	Topic

ADDITIONAL NOTES

_____

_____

_____

_____

_____

_____

_____

_____

_____

FAMILY MEETING
Creating Healthy Family Communication

Time Began: _____ Ended: _____ Led by: _____ Date: _____

Announcements: _____

_____

_____

Topic Examples: Family activities, family problems, standards, motivational systems, and consequences.

Rules: No pointing fingers, name calling, etc. Topics should never target a person. Those issues can be discussed in mentor meetings. When discussing rationales, decisions and benefits, keep top-of-mind: Fair, effective, love and concern, pleasant atmosphere.

Topic 1: _____ Rationales: _____

Suggestions:
1. _____ 2. _____

_____ _____

3. _____ 4. _____

_____ _____

Vote   1. Yes __ / No __   2. Yes __ / No __   3. Yes __ / No __   4. Yes __ / No __

Decision: _____ Benefit: _____

Topic 2: _____ Rationales: _____

Suggestions:
1. _____ 2. _____

_____ _____

3. _____ 4. _____

_____ _____

Vote   1. Yes __ / No __   2. Yes __ / No __   3. Yes __ / No __   4. Yes __ / No __

Decision: _____ Benefit: _____

Family Meetings should create a tone of peace, communication, order, justice, freedom, and safety

TOPICS TO BE DISCUSSED AT THE NEXT MEETING

	Date / Name	Topic

ADDITIONAL NOTES

_____

_____

_____

_____

_____

_____

_____

_____

_____

FAMILY MEETING

Creating Healthy Family Communication

Time Began: _____ Ended: _____ Led by: _____ Date: _____

Announcements: _____

_____

_____

Topic Examples: Family activities, family problems, standards, motivational systems, and consequences.

Rules: No pointing fingers, name calling, etc. Topics should never target a person. Those issues can be discussed in mentor meetings. When discussing rationales, decisions and benefits, keep top-of-mind: Fair, effective, love and concern, pleasant atmosphere.

Topic 1: _____ Rationales: _____

Suggestions:

1. _____ 2. _____

_____ _____

3. _____ 4. _____

_____ _____

Vote   1. Yes __ / No __   2. Yes __ / No __   3. Yes __ / No __   4. Yes __ / No __

Decision: _____ Benefit: _____

Topic 2: _____ Rationales: _____

Suggestions:

1. _____ 2. _____

_____ _____

3. _____ 4. _____

_____ _____

Vote   1. Yes __ / No __   2. Yes __ / No __   3. Yes __ / No __   4. Yes __ / No __

Decision: _____ Benefit: _____

Family Meetings should create a tone of peace, communication, order, justice, freedom, and safety

TOPICS TO BE DISCUSSED AT THE NEXT MEETING

	Date / Name	Topic

ADDITIONAL NOTES

FAMILY MEETING

Creating Healthy Family Communication

Time Began: _____ Ended: _____ Led by: _____ Date: _____

Announcements: _____

_____

_____

Topic Examples: Family activities, family problems, standards, motivational systems, and consequences.

Rules: No pointing fingers, name calling, etc. Topics should never target a person. Those issues can be discussed in mentor meetings. When discussing rationales, decisions and benefits, keep top-of-mind: Fair, effective, love and concern, pleasant atmosphere.

Topic 1: _____ Rationales: _____

Suggestions:

1. _____   2. _____

_____   _____

3. _____   4. _____

_____   _____

Vote   1. Yes __ / No __   2. Yes __ / No __   3. Yes __ / No __   4. Yes __ / No __

Decision: _____ Benefit: _____

Topic 2: _____ Rationales: _____

Suggestions:

1. _____   2. _____

_____   _____

3. _____   4. _____

_____   _____

Vote   1. Yes __ / No __   2. Yes __ / No __   3. Yes __ / No __   4. Yes __ / No __

Decision: _____ Benefit: _____

Family Meetings should create a tone of peace, communication, order, justice, freedom, and safety

TOPICS TO BE DISCUSSED AT THE NEXT MEETING

	Date / Name	Topic

ADDITIONAL NOTES

FAMILY MEETING
Creating Healthy Family Communication

Time Began: _____ Ended: _____ Led by: _____ Date: _____

Announcements: _____

_____

_____

Topic Examples: Family activities, family problems, standards, motivational systems, and consequences.

Rules: No pointing fingers, name calling, etc. Topics should never target a person. Those issues can be discussed in mentor meetings. When discussing rationales, decisions and benefits, keep top-of-mind: Fair, effective, love and concern, pleasant atmosphere.

Topic 1: _____ Rationales: _____

Suggestions:

1. _____   2. _____

_____   _____

3. _____   4. _____

_____   _____

Vote   1. Yes __ / No __   2. Yes __ / No __   3. Yes __ / No __   4. Yes __ / No __

Decision: _____ Benefit: _____

Topic 2: _____ Rationales: _____

Suggestions:

1. _____   2. _____

_____   _____

3. _____   4. _____

_____   _____

Vote   1. Yes __ / No __   2. Yes __ / No __   3. Yes __ / No __   4. Yes __ / No __

Decision: _____ Benefit: _____

Family Meetings should create a tone of peace, communication, order, justice, freedom, and safety

TOPICS TO BE DISCUSSED AT THE NEXT MEETING

	Date / Name	Topic

ADDITIONAL NOTES

_____

_____

_____

_____

_____

_____

_____

_____

_____

FAMILY MEETING

Creating Healthy Family Communication

Time Began: _____ Ended: _____ Led by: _____ Date: _____

Announcements: _____

_____

_____

Topic Examples: Family activities, family problems, standards, motivational systems, and consequences.

Rules: No pointing fingers, name calling, etc. Topics should never target a person. Those issues can be discussed in mentor meetings. When discussing rationales, decisions and benefits, keep top-of-mind: Fair, effective, love and concern, pleasant atmosphere.

Topic 1: _____ Rationales: _____

Suggestions:

1. _____ 2. _____

_____ _____

3. _____ 4. _____

_____ _____

Vote   1. Yes __ / No __   2. Yes __ / No __   3. Yes __ / No __   4. Yes __ / No __

Decision: _____ Benefit: _____

Topic 2: _____ Rationales: _____

Suggestions:

1. _____ 2. _____

_____ _____

3. _____ 4. _____

_____ _____

Vote   1. Yes __ / No __   2. Yes __ / No __   3. Yes __ / No __   4. Yes __ / No __

Decision: _____ Benefit: _____

Family Meetings should create a tone of peace, communication, order, justice, freedom, and safety

TOPICS TO BE DISCUSSED AT THE NEXT MEETING

	Date / Name	Topic

ADDITIONAL NOTES

FAMILY MEETING

Creating Healthy Family Communication

Time Began: _____ Ended: _____ Led by: _____ Date: _____

Announcements: _____

_____

_____

Topic Examples: Family activities, family problems, standards, motivational systems, and consequences.

Rules: No pointing fingers, name calling, etc. Topics should never target a person. Those issues can be discussed in mentor meetings. When discussing rationales, decisions and benefits, keep top-of-mind: Fair, effective, love and concern, pleasant atmosphere.

Topic 1: _____ Rationales: _____

Suggestions:

1. _____   2. _____

_____   _____

3. _____   4. _____

_____   _____

Vote   1. Yes __ / No __   2. Yes __ / No __   3. Yes __ / No __   4. Yes __ / No __

Decision: _____ Benefit: _____

Topic 2: _____ Rationales: _____

Suggestions:

1. _____   2. _____

_____   _____

3. _____   4. _____

_____   _____

Vote   1. Yes __ / No __   2. Yes __ / No __   3. Yes __ / No __   4. Yes __ / No __

Decision: _____ Benefit: _____

Family Meetings should create a tone of peace, communication, order, justice, freedom, and safety

TOPICS TO BE DISCUSSED AT THE NEXT MEETING

	Date / Name	Topic

ADDITIONAL NOTES

FAMILY MEETING

Creating Healthy Family Communication

Time Began: _____ Ended: _____ Led by: _____ Date: _____

Announcements: _____

_____

_____

Topic Examples: Family activities, family problems, standards, motivational systems, and consequences.

Rules: No pointing fingers, name calling, etc. Topics should never target a person. Those issues can be discussed in mentor meetings. When discussing rationales, decisions and benefits, keep top-of-mind: Fair, effective, love and concern, pleasant atmosphere.

Topic 1: _____ Rationales: _____

Suggestions:

1. _____   2. _____

_____   _____

3. _____   4. _____

_____   _____

Vote   1. Yes __ / No __   2. Yes __ / No __   3. Yes __ / No __   4. Yes __ / No __

Decision: _____ Benefit: _____

Topic 2: _____ Rationales: _____

Suggestions:

1. _____   2. _____

_____   _____

3. _____   4. _____

_____   _____

Vote   1. Yes __ / No __   2. Yes __ / No __   3. Yes __ / No __   4. Yes __ / No __

Decision: _____ Benefit: _____

Family Meetings should create a tone of peace, communication, order, justice, freedom, and safety

TOPICS TO BE DISCUSSED AT THE NEXT MEETING

	Date / Name	Topic

ADDITIONAL NOTES

FAMILY MEETING

Creating Healthy Family Communication

Time Began: _____ Ended: _____ Led by: _____ Date: _____

Announcements: _____

_____

_____

Topic Examples: Family activities, family problems, standards, motivational systems, and consequences.

Rules: No pointing fingers, name calling, etc. Topics should never target a person. Those issues can be discussed in mentor meetings. When discussing rationales, decisions and benefits, keep top-of-mind: Fair, effective, love and concern, pleasant atmosphere.

Topic 1: _____ Rationales: _____

Suggestions:

1. _____ 2. _____

_____ _____

3. _____ 4. _____

_____ _____

Vote   1. Yes __ / No __   2. Yes __ / No __   3. Yes __ / No __   4. Yes __ / No __

Decision: _____ Benefit: _____

Topic 2: _____ Rationales: _____

Suggestions:

1. _____ 2. _____

_____ _____

3. _____ 4. _____

_____ _____

Vote   1. Yes __ / No __   2. Yes __ / No __   3. Yes __ / No __   4. Yes __ / No __

Decision: _____ Benefit: _____

Family Meetings should create a tone of peace, communication, order, justice, freedom, and safety

TOPICS TO BE DISCUSSED AT THE NEXT MEETING

	Date / Name	Topic

ADDITIONAL NOTES

FAMILY MEETING

Creating Healthy Family Communication

Time Began: _____ Ended: _____ Led by: _____ Date: _____

Announcements: _____

_____

_____

Topic Examples: Family activities, family problems, standards, motivational systems, and consequences.

Rules: No pointing fingers, name calling, etc. Topics should never target a person. Those issues can be discussed in mentor meetings. When discussing rationales, decisions and benefits, keep top-of-mind: Fair, effective, love and concern, pleasant atmosphere.

Topic 1: _____ Rationales: _____

Suggestions:

1. _____   2. _____

   _____   _____

3. _____   4. _____

   _____   _____

Vote   1. Yes __ / No __   2. Yes __ / No __   3. Yes __ / No __   4. Yes __ / No __

Decision: _____ Benefit: _____

Topic 2: _____ Rationales: _____

Suggestions:

1. _____   2. _____

   _____   _____

3. _____   4. _____

   _____   _____

Vote   1. Yes __ / No __   2. Yes __ / No __   3. Yes __ / No __   4. Yes __ / No __

Decision: _____ Benefit: _____

Family Meetings should create a tone of peace, communication, order, justice, freedom, and safety

TOPICS TO BE DISCUSSED AT THE NEXT MEETING

	Date / Name	Topic

ADDITIONAL NOTES

FAMILY MEETING

Creating Healthy Family Communication

Time Began: _____ Ended: _____ Led by: _____ Date: _____

Announcements: _____

_____

_____

Topic Examples: Family activities, family problems, standards, motivational systems, and consequences.

Rules: No pointing fingers, name calling, etc. Topics should never target a person. Those issues can be discussed in mentor meetings. When discussing rationales, decisions and benefits, keep top-of-mind: Fair, effective, love and concern, pleasant atmosphere.

Topic 1: _____ Rationales: _____

Suggestions:

1. _____   2. _____

_____   _____

3. _____   4. _____

_____   _____

Vote   1. Yes __ / No __   2. Yes __ / No __   3. Yes __ / No __   4. Yes __ / No __

Decision: _____ Benefit: _____

Topic 2: _____ Rationales: _____

Suggestions:

1. _____   2. _____

_____   _____

3. _____   4. _____

_____   _____

Vote   1. Yes __ / No __   2. Yes __ / No __   3. Yes __ / No __   4. Yes __ / No __

Decision: _____ Benefit: _____

Family Meetings should create a tone of peace, communication, order, justice, freedom, and safety

TOPICS TO BE DISCUSSED AT THE NEXT MEETING

	Date / Name	Topic

ADDITIONAL NOTES

FAMILY MEETING

Creating Healthy Family Communication

Time Began: _____ Ended: _____ Led by: _____ Date: _____

Announcements: _____

_____

_____

Topic Examples: Family activities, family problems, standards, motivational systems, and consequences.

Rules: No pointing fingers, name calling, etc. Topics should never target a person. Those issues can be discussed in mentor meetings. When discussing rationales, decisions and benefits, keep top-of-mind: Fair, effective, love and concern, pleasant atmosphere.

Topic 1: _____ Rationales: _____

Suggestions:
1. _____   2. _____

3. _____   4. _____

Vote   1. Yes __ / No __   2. Yes __ / No __   3. Yes __ / No __   4. Yes __ / No __

Decision: _____ Benefit: _____

Topic 2: _____ Rationales: _____

Suggestions:
1. _____   2. _____

3. _____   4. _____

Vote   1. Yes __ / No __   2. Yes __ / No __   3. Yes __ / No __   4. Yes __ / No __

Decision: _____ Benefit: _____

Family Meetings should create a tone of peace, communication, order, justice, freedom, and safety

TOPICS TO BE DISCUSSED AT THE NEXT MEETING

	Date / Name	Topic

ADDITIONAL NOTES

FAMILY MEETING
Creating Healthy Family Communication

Time Began: _____ Ended: _____ Led by: _____ Date: _____

Announcements: _____

_____

_____

Topic Examples: Family activities, family problems, standards, motivational systems, and consequences.

Rules: No pointing fingers, name calling, etc. Topics should never target a person. Those issues can be discussed in mentor meetings. When discussing rationales, decisions and benefits, keep top-of-mind: Fair, effective, love and concern, pleasant atmosphere.

Topic 1: _____ Rationales: _____

Suggestions:

1. _____   2. _____

_____   _____

3. _____   4. _____

_____   _____

Vote   1. Yes __ / No __   2. Yes __ / No __   3. Yes __ / No __   4. Yes __ / No __

Decision: _____ Benefit: _____

Topic 2: _____ Rationales: _____

Suggestions:

1. _____   2. _____

_____   _____

3. _____   4. _____

_____   _____

Vote   1. Yes __ / No __   2. Yes __ / No __   3. Yes __ / No __   4. Yes __ / No __

Decision: _____ Benefit: _____

Family Meetings should create a tone of peace, communication, order, justice, freedom, and safety

TOPICS TO BE DISCUSSED AT THE NEXT MEETING

	Date / Name	Topic

ADDITIONAL NOTES

FAMILY MEETING
Creating Healthy Family Communication

Time Began: _____ Ended: _____ Led by: _____ Date: _____

Announcements: _____

_____

_____

Topic Examples: Family activities, family problems, standards, motivational systems, and consequences.

Rules: No pointing fingers, name calling, etc. Topics should never target a person. Those issues can be discussed in mentor meetings. When discussing rationales, decisions and benefits, keep top-of-mind: Fair, effective, love and concern, pleasant atmosphere.

Topic 1: _____ Rationales: _____

Suggestions:

1. _____   2. _____

_____   _____

3. _____   4. _____

_____   _____

Vote   1. Yes __ / No __   2. Yes __ / No __   3. Yes __ / No __   4. Yes __ / No __

Decision: _____ Benefit: _____

Topic 2: _____ Rationales: _____

Suggestions:

1. _____   2. _____

_____   _____

3. _____   4. _____

_____   _____

Vote   1. Yes __ / No __   2. Yes __ / No __   3. Yes __ / No __   4. Yes __ / No __

Decision: _____ Benefit: _____

Family Meetings should create a tone of peace, communication, order, justice, freedom, and safety

TOPICS TO BE DISCUSSED AT THE NEXT MEETING

	Date / Name	Topic

ADDITIONAL NOTES

FAMILY MEETING
Creating Healthy Family Communication

Time Began: _____ Ended: _____ Led by: _____ Date: _____

Announcements: _____

_____

_____

Topic Examples: Family activities, family problems, standards, motivational systems, and consequences.

Rules: No pointing fingers, name calling, etc. Topics should never target a person. Those issues can be discussed in mentor meetings. When discussing rationales, decisions and benefits, keep top-of-mind: Fair, effective, love and concern, pleasant atmosphere.

Topic 1: _____ Rationales: _____

Suggestions:

1. _____   2. _____

_____   _____

3. _____   4. _____

_____   _____

Vote   1. Yes __ / No __   2. Yes __ / No __   3. Yes __ / No __   4. Yes __ / No __

Decision: _____ Benefit: _____

Topic 2: _____ Rationales: _____

Suggestions:

1. _____   2. _____

_____   _____

3. _____   4. _____

_____   _____

Vote   1. Yes __ / No __   2. Yes __ / No __   3. Yes __ / No __   4. Yes __ / No __

Decision: _____ Benefit: _____

Family Meetings should create a tone of peace, communication, order, justice, freedom, and safety

TOPICS TO BE DISCUSSED AT THE NEXT MEETING

	Date / Name	Topic

ADDITIONAL NOTES

FAMILY MEETING

Creating Healthy Family Communication

Time Began: _____ Ended: _____ Led by: _____ Date: _____

Announcements: _____

_____

_____

Topic Examples: Family activities, family problems, standards, motivational systems, and consequences.

Rules: No pointing fingers, name calling, etc. Topics should never target a person. Those issues can be discussed in mentor meetings. When discussing rationales, decisions and benefits, keep top-of-mind: Fair, effective, love and concern, pleasant atmosphere.

Topic 1: _____ Rationales: _____

Suggestions:

1. _____   2. _____

_____   _____

3. _____   4. _____

_____   _____

Vote   1. Yes ___ / No ___   2. Yes ___ / No ___   3. Yes ___ / No ___   4. Yes ___ / No ___

Decision: _____ Benefit: _____

Topic 2: _____ Rationales: _____

Suggestions:

1. _____   2. _____

_____   _____

3. _____   4. _____

_____   _____

Vote   1. Yes ___ / No ___   2. Yes ___ / No ___   3. Yes ___ / No ___   4. Yes ___ / No ___

Decision: _____ Benefit: _____

Family Meetings should create a tone of peace, communication, order, justice, freedom, and safety

ABOUT THE AUTHOR

When it comes to parenting, Nicholeen Peck is a worldwide phenomenon and leader — and for good reason! Her proven system based on Four Simple Skills transforms even the most out-of-control teenagers and homes from chaos to calm within days. Though she's an international speaker, author, mentor, former foster parent of many difficult and troubled teens, and even President of the Worldwide Organization for Women (an approved consultant for the United Nations), Nicholeen spends most of her time at home with her husband and four children, which she knows will be her greatest impact and legacy. The fact that she has such an international influence while still being a stay-at-home mom is evidence of the effectiveness of her teachings. Learn more about her mission and methods at www.teachingselfgovernment.com.

RESOURCES TO IMPLEMENT
TEACHING SELF-GOVERNMENT PRINCIPLES
IN YOUR HOME

If you want help implementing the Teaching Self-Government principles into your home, or would like more understanding of how it all works --

The Teaching Self-Government IMPLEMENTATION COURSE™ is just for you!

The Implementation Course includes:
- Advanced Level Classes
- Video of actual parenting interactions
- Weekly group mentor calls with Nicholeen
- A special member forum for Q&A
- Ongoing supportive

Buy the full course at:
http://teachingselfgovernment.com/store

Also available at **http://teachingingselfgovernment.com**:
- Audio Classes
- Family Tutorial DVD of the Aponte family learning Teaching Self-Government
- TSG Circle memberships
- TSG Weekly Support Group
- Children's books
- Cue Cards
- Poster of the Choices Map
- Books
- and more...

Made in the USA
Columbia, SC
23 November 2021

49550683R00117